Regrounding a Pilgrimage

by
JOHN MATTHIAS & JOHN PECK

Introduction by Robert Archambeau
Edited by Katie Lehman

DOS MADRES
2018

DOS MADRES PRESS INC.
P.O.Box 294, Loveland, Ohio 45140
www.dosmadres.com editor@dosmadres.com

Dos Madres is dedicated to the belief that the small press is essential to the vitality of contemporary literature as a carrier of the new voice, as well as the older, sometimes forgotten voices of the past. And in an ever more virtual world, to the creation of fine books pleasing to the eye and hand.

Dos Madres is named in honor of Vera Murphy and Libbie Hughes, the "Dos Madres" whose contributions have made this press possible.

Dos Madres Press, Inc. is an Ohio Not For Profit Corporation and a 501 (c) (3) qualified public charity. Contributions are tax deductible.

Executive Editor: Robert J. Murphy

Illustration & Book Design: Elizabeth H. Murphy
www.illusionstudios.net

Typeset in Adobe Garamond Pro & Celtic Garamond the 2nd
ISBN 978-1-948017-29-9
Library of Congress Control Number: 2018959019

First Edition

Copyright 2018 John Matthias & John Peck
All rights reserved. No part of this book may be reproduced or transmitted in any form or by any means graphic, electronic or mechanical, including photocopying, recording, taping or by any information storage or retrieval system, without the permission in writing from the publisher.

Published by Dos Madres Press, Inc.

ACKNOWLEDGEMENTS

Early versions of "A Compostela Diptych" have appeared previously in four books by John Matthias: *A Gathering of Ways* (Swallow Press, 1991), *Beltane at Aphelion* (Swallow Press, 1995), *New Selected Poems* (Salt, 2004), and *Collected Longer Poems* (Shearsman Books, 2012). A shorter version of John Peck's essay first appeared in *Word Play Place: Essays on the Poetry of John Matthias*, ed. Robert Archambeau (Swallow Press, 1998). Robert Archambeau's essay first appeared in *Inventions of a Barbarous Age: Poetry from Conceptualism to Rhyme* (MadHat Press, 2016).

In memory of
David Jones, Robert Duncan & Guy Davenport

*

There are two voices, and the first voice says, "Write!"
and the second voice says, "For whom?"
I think that's marvelous;
he doesn't question the imperative, you see that.
And the first voice says,
"For the dead whom thou didst love";
again the second voice doesn't question it;
instead it says, "Will they read me?"
And the first voice says,
"Aye, for they return as posterity." Isn't that good?

(Hamann, quoted by Kierkegaard, quoted by Berryman)

TABLE OF CONTENTS

Foreword
— 1 —

Introduction
Robert Archambeau
— 7 —

A Compostela Diptych
John Matthias
— 17 —

Epilogue
John Matthias
— 81 —

Agensay, Agengrownde, Matthias
John Peck
— 89 —

FOREWORD

Robert Archambeau began to imagine an edition of essays on the poetry of John Matthias in 1995 while listening to a panel on Matthias's work at the annual conference of the American Comparative Literature Association held at Notre Dame. By 1998, when Archambeau's book appeared as *Word Play Place*, thirteen essays were in place. One piece seemed so remarkable that Matthias told Archambeau that he immediately imagined it as a companion to some future reprint of the Compostela section of his earlier book *A Gathering of Ways*. The essay in question was John Peck's "Petitio, Repetitio, Agensay, Agengrownde, Matthias." When he first read the piece, Matthias phoned Archambeau to say, "Peck's essay is better than the poem itself."

Regrounding a Pilgrimage is nothing less than the fruition of that vision and something else entirely. An engaging companion indeed, the book offers the pieces—verse and prose—as a kind of inventive dialogue with Matthias's "A Compostela Diptych" at its center. Matthias's poem traces the routes, both geographically and historically, of the Camino de Santiago (the Way of St. James) leading to the shrine of St. James in northwest Spain. Dating back to ninth-century Galicia with the discovery of remains believed, although later disputed, to be that of St. James the Apostle, pilgrims began traveling along a network of roads, some built in the time of the Roman Empire, others by "strangers and their armies," to the tomb, and later cathedral, of Santiago de Compostela. From France medieval pilgrims traveled four major routes: the Via Tolosana (the Way of Arles), the Via

Podiensis (the Way of Le Puy-en-Velay), the Via Turonensis (the Way of Tours), and Via Lemosina (the Way of Vézaley).

The allure of pilgrimage to Santiago has outlasted the debate around the authenticity of the remains, with present-day pilgrims traveling similar routes through southern France and northern Spain, following in the footsteps of thousands of pilgrim predecessors, and for Matthias, who in 1987 walked parts of the Via Tolosana, those others along the way and wayside—lepers, soldiers, scribes, heretics.

In two parts, from France and from Spain, Matthias time-travels an expansive religious and political history, from pre-Christian pilgrims following the Milky Way to Finisterre—the westernmost point on the Iberian Peninsula believed to be the end of the world—to subsequent Christian pilgrims who journeyed to Finisterre en route to Santiago to collect a scallop shell as token of their pilgrimage. One finds Muslim conquerors during the Umayyad Conquest and soldiers of Charlemagne. Not to be forgotten is the twelfth-century influx of pilgrims following the *Codex Calixtinus,* a pilgrim's guide attributed to French monk and scholar Aimery Picaud. Of the litany of "travelers" in "A Compostela Diptych," whether self-described pilgrims or figures of history, Matthias includes, among others, Priscillian (ca. 385), Abd-al-Rahman I (731–788), Charlemagne (742–814), Abd-al-Rahman II (792–852), the monks of Cluny, of St. Victor in Marseille, and of Chamalières, Almanzor (938–1002), Rodrigo Díaz El Campeador (1043–1099), Alfonso VI of Castile (1043–1109), Abbot Suger (1081–1151), and Napoleon Bonaparte (1769–1821).

In "A Compostela Diptych," a historical tangling and poetic untangling of time periods and events occur on both literal geographical ground and through a historical nonground, that is, through immaterial, or memory, regrounded, says Peck, by Matthias poetically. In the aforemetioned essay "Petitio, Repetitio, Agensay, Agengrownde, Matthias," revised here as "Agensay, Agengrownde, Matthias," Peck, a Jungian analyst as well as poet, notes that this poetic regrounding in "A Compostela Diptych" is set up in part through Matthias's earlier work, for instance, in "A Wind in Rousillon," in which "anamnesis and literal place pass through the other place or topos of feminine breath." As he does in "A Wind in Rousillon," Matthias in "A Compostela Diptych" employs a "dialectical sieve of neutral care"—the sieve being litany—which "collects and arranges atrocities" in an attempt at full recollection. This is the poet's work of coming to terms with ground—both a greater *chora* and a literal ground, including the histories enacted there, and one's place "there"—a nonlocatable ground—which, according to Peck, Matthias turns over with piercing sharpness, a care that is comprehensive and without illusion. Stripped of sentimental reminiscence, Matthias almost methodically lists, unattached, fixed particulars while moving through them and creating movement poetically in them by way of the old forms of refrain and repetition.

"There was a time," notes Peck, when "inner grounding could be trudged out," when "cultural morale could imaginally contain the ragged yet bold idea of an overarching culture by covering the ground on foot." Matthias details all that Western Europe has done and undone on those grounds by way of a progression of poetic constructions of varied repetition. Similarly

Matthias uses refrain, according to Peck, not as closure but as process, "anticipating retotalization or renewed return." He does so not by requiring language to be self-contained, as literal ground, or by submitting to the authority of linguistic operations, as opposed to linguistic universals, at the insistence of Language poetry, but through a penetrative form that challenges the memory of ground through his exploration of poetic voice. With the munitions blast that appears in the last section of "A Compostela Diptych," Matthias clears away the "patient inventory without disaffirming what it clears away." In this way Matthias maintains equilibrium through tension between the "older poetics of climax and catharsis" and "the modernist rupture of it" without becoming, according to Peck, absorbed by either compositional impulse. The effect lends itself to the regrounding of poetic speech, and thus enables a conceptual regrounding of poetry's historical and at times personal situations.

As Archambeau mentions in his introduction, the totalization of history as presented by Matthias in "A Compostela Diptych" can be seen in a Levinasian sense, in which "diverse elements are reduced to the same manifestations of a single force"—one of catastrophe after catastrophe—which Matthias escapes, albeit briefly, into Gnosticism, "only"—abundantly—to return to the infinite historical particulars that fill the poet-traveler's journey. These particulars *take place*—if we must have a place, notes Peck—through speech, and even through the absence of speech, for example, in the "post-blast quiet," a "deafening sound" that nods to primordial silence. Through his inventory of Western European discord, according to Peck,

Matthias "transits Christian hope while touching the sad contradictions of political Christendom, to bank on hope rather than with any of its formulae." This silence and hope, Peck says, "bypasses the individual heart and the mystic's privacy" for the "*silentium* and *spes* derived from collective experience." Through speech and silence, Matthias makes way for an unfixed but persistent historical memory by his repeated progressions that create the "nonplace of our meeting"—a communal meeting, left untethered, of all who have come before and who will come after.

Sound is the means by which Matthias listens to his own words to find ground. He probes the shallows with a kedging oar to "enter history" in his later "Kedging in Time." Through sounding as listening, notes Peck, the poet attends to the "nonobvious enterprise of grounding himself." He does this elsewhere in previous works, in "East Anglian Diptych" and "Northern Summer," as a transatlantic American, and in his recent collaboration *Revolutions*. Grounding oneself through sound figures most notably in "A Compostela Diptych" when Matthias suffers both illness and loss during the time of its writing.

The pilgrimage, both on foot and in words, then, becomes personal where the poetic and autobiographical converge. The epilogue speaks directly to this inner quest in acknowledging the "primal, secret, terrified & universal query of the sick: "*What did I do wrong / to suffer this?*" / While "A Compostela Diptych" does not end at either the pilgrimage destination of Santiago or the wholeness of the veteran traveler, or even, as Archambeau notes, at a totalized vision of history, the epilogue suspends itself in that terrified question into suffering begun by "A

Compostela Diptych" through the pilgrim-poet's continued movement forward anticipating completion.

> And that Santiago, call him what you like,
> Son of Thunder, Good Saint Jacques, The Fisherman,
>
> Or whoever really lies there—
> hermit, heretic, shaman healer with no name—
> will somehow make us whole.

Katie Lehman

INTRODUCTION
by Robert Archambeau

A Gathering of Ways is a suite of poems centering on the act of pilgrimage—and therefore, one might reasonably assume, the poem of a pilgrim, on his way to a sacred place for sacred purposes.[1] But John Matthias is a funny sort of pilgrim. We have it, after all, on the best of authorities that the poetry of John Matthias has heretical tendencies. Here's what Robert Duncan said about Matthias in an undated letter from the early 1970s:

> Matthias is a goliard—one of those wandering souls out of a Dark Age in our own time . . . carrying with him as he goes in his pack of cards certain key cards that come ever into his hand when he plays: the juggler (as he was to be portrayed later in the Tarot), the scholar whose head is filled with learning and the fame of amorous women and the heretic remembering witch-hunts yet to come.

A goliard! Already Matthias is in trouble, the goliards being clerical students of the Middle Ages who affirmed the flesh and derided the corruption of Mother Church.

---

1   This essay was originally published as "History, Totality, Silence" in Robert Archambeau's *Inventions of a Barbarous Age: Poetry from Conceptualism to Rhyme* (Asheville, NC: MadHat Press, 2016).

And not just any goliard, but a goliard Duncan associates with the juggler of the Tarot (in esoteric decks, a figure for the magus who masters dark arts) and with the heretic seeing into a future of persecutions. We may as well call in Torquemada's inquisition and get this heretic burning over with. But Duncan is talking about the Matthias of the sixties and early seventies, and thinking of Matthias's political radicalism and of his early obsessions with alchemy and witchcraft. What of the Matthias of the later Matthias?

Consider three long poems of Matthias's that form a poetic suite: "An East Anglian Diptych," "Facts from an Apocryphal Midwest," and "A Compostela Diptych," written between 1984 and 1990, and published collectively as *A Gathering of Ways*. The general project of the poems indicates a turning-away from the Matthias described by Duncan: they are attempts of coming to terms with what Matthias called his "post-activist consternation" and alienation from American life. "An East Anglian Diptych" is Matthias's attempt to make a psychological home for himself in England, and "Facts from an Apocryphal Midwest" represents a similar home-making project in America. This is no longer the radical wanderer, but the poet in search of stability. Indeed, "A Compostela Diptych," takes as its subject the ancient pilgrim routes across France and Spain to Santiago de Compostela. It's an attempt by the post-activist Matthias to come to terms with, and possibly make himself at home in, both the history of the West and the dominant spiritual tradition of the West, Catholicism.

But to what terms does he come? If I were to try to sum them up, I'd say this: in "A Compostela Diptych," Matthias attempts to present a totalized history of the West and of Catholicism. But he fails to find a happy totality, and this drives him toward an otherworldly yearning, a yearning for a world beyond history, an eternal world free of violence. This is essentially a Gnostic yearning for some eternal, infinite elsewhere of light, a yearning from which he only escapes at the very end of the poem.

When I speak of a "totalized history" in "A Compostela Diptych," I want to use the term "totality" in a vaguely Levinasian sense: as something finite, in which diverse elements are reduced to "the violently pacified empire of Same" or "the counted-as-one" (to use Dominic Fox's glosses for Levinas's "totality"). With regard to history, we can think of totalization as the opposite of an unending series of discrete events—the opposite, that is, of Henry Ford's version of history as "one damn thing after another"—or perhaps we can think of it as the hammering of such discrete phenomena into something whole, in which apparently disparate parts are in fact manifestations of a single force, or repetitions of a single pattern. We're on the same page about this if you're thinking of one of the most famous passages in the works of Walter Benjamin, which reads:

> A Klee painting named *Angelus Novus* shows an angel looking as though he is about to move away from something he is fixedly contemplating. His eyes are staring, his mouth is open, his wings

are spread. This is how one pictures the angel of history. His face is turned toward the past. Where we perceive a chain of events, he sees one single catastrophe which keeps piling wreckage upon wreckage and hurls it in front of his feet. The angel would like to stay, awaken the dead, and make whole what has been smashed. But a storm is blowing from Paradise; it has got caught in his wings with such violence that the angel can no longer close them. The storm irresistibly propels him into the future to which his back is turned, while the pile of debris before him grows skyward.

This is a vision of history as total, and as total disaster. And this is very much the vision of history that Matthias gives us in "A Compostela Diptych."

It doesn't seem that way at first, though. "A Compostela Diptych" begins with what seems to be a happy vision of the many pilgrims who have trodden the various routes through France and Spain to the cathedral at Santiago de Compostela. There's a barrage of proper names of people and places: some forty-one different proper names in the first forty-five lines of the poem. On the face of it, this doesn't seem like the writing of a man who would present history as a totality. Nothing, after all, insists on irreducible specificity more than a proper name. Indeed, proper names will be very significant at the end of the poem, when Matthias shakes himself free of a totalized version of history—but I'm getting ahead of myself. The point I want to make here doesn't have to do with proper names, but with a collective pronoun, "they." Unlike proper names, collective pronouns reduce the many to the one, and what we see happen in the opening of "A Compostela Diptych" is a reduction of the people of different European nations and centuries into a single, collective, "they"—a trans-historical subject for the people of Catholic Europe. Here we have the multitudes "counted-as-one." It doesn't seem, at first, to be anything but a joyous affair, a holy journey uniting the many. But this all changes a few pages into the poem. After Matthias gestures toward the song of the pilgrims, he adds this:

> And there was other song—song sung inwardly
> to a percussion of the jangling
> manacles and fetters hanging on the branded
>
> heretics who crawled the roads
> on hands and knees and slept with lepers under
> dark façades of abbeys
>
> & the west portals of cathedrals . . .

There is a dissonance in the happy totality of history: those who do not fit, those who are expelled, despised, oppressed. This is a vision of the violence of the totality, and soon the history his poem recounts becomes a history of crusade, jihad, and inquisition, while a small minority yearns for an escape into timeless peace. Indeed, history becomes totalized in a new way—as Benjamin's totality of "one single catastrophe which keeps piling wreckage upon wreckage."

Matthias creates a sense of this catastrophic historical totality through four main techniques. I call them coincidence in place; rhyming actions; musical refrain; and musical reprise.

Coincidence in place presents history as total catastrophe by giving us a series of almost archeological sections in which the same geography hosts similar events over time. For example, Matthias shows us Charlemagne's minions slaughtered during a crusade in Spain. These events coincide in space with later massacres of the Spanish Inquisition centuries later, and with still later massacres perpetuated by Napoleon in the Peninsular War. We dig into the history of particular places, and, like Benjamin's angel, see only wreckage piling upon wreckage.

By "rhyming actions" I mean historical events that Matthias presents as essentially parallel. Notable among these is the fate of the cathedral bells of Santiago. Early in the poem we see these hauled away by the conquering armies of Islamic Spain under Almanzor, who hangs them upside down in his great mosque and uses them as candelabra. Much later in the poem and in history we see Alfonso VI of Castile sack the mosque and take the bells back to Santiago, installing them in the cathedral for their original use. The effect of these actions, which echo one another, is to remind the reader of conflict, and of the hubris of conquerors, as the constants of history.

There are many refrains in "A Compostela Diptych," but among the most resonant refrains is the phrase "darkness fell at noon." We hear it at many moments in the poem when political disaster falls. The refrain not only serves to unite these moments—it also connects those moments to more modern disasters. *Darkness at Noon* is, after all, the title of Arthur Koestler's novel about the evils of Stalinism.

    Musical reprise is a technique quite common in opera and musical drama, but unusual in poetry: the passing of the same lyrical part from one voice to another in different contexts. A number of different passages get a reprise in "A Compostela Diptych," but the most insistent one is Charlemagne's dream of war, an eighteen-line passage lifted from the *Chanson de Roland*. We're first given it as a prophetic dream in the mind of Charlemagne, but we hear it again, in whole or in part, in the voices of other characters (notably Aimery Picaud, the chronicler of the pilgrim routes, and John Moore, the English general killed while fighting Napoleon's armies at Corunna), or with reference to other conflicts, including modern acts of terrorism by Basque separatists. The effect of the reprise is to make all of history into Charlemagne's nightmare of war—a nightmare from which we seem unable to wake up.

    Not that some characters in Matthias's poem don't try. Accompanying the long nightmare of history recounted in "A Compostela Diptych" is another story, a story of Gnostics who long for a world beyond this broken, bruised, and evil one in which we seem perpetually imprisoned. This group includes the historical Gnostics and heretics of the times and places covered by the poem (Cathars, Albigensians, and the like). But Matthias interprets Gnosticism broadly, and includes in it the Eleusinian mysteries, the practitioners of the medieval Trobar Clus, and the Sufi mystics of Islamic Spain. He even includes Ezra Pound, wandering as a young man through the south of France, and dreaming of a light beyond the nightmare and wreckage of history.

There is much in "A Compostela Diptych" to indicate that Matthias would join with the Gnostic tradition, especially in the poem's final section. Here, Matthias presents us with a moment where we seem to leave history, and indeed this world, behind, in an intersection of the timeless with time. The occasion for the intersection is the explosion of an enormous Spanish armory, an explosion that shakes foundations and, from many miles away, creates shockwaves that ring the Santiago cathedral bells, the same ones that had been hauled away by conquering Moors and hauled back by crusaders. Now, we're told

                                    men

    whose job it was to ring them stood
    amazed out in the square & wondered if this thunder
    and the ringing was in time for Vespers

    or for Nones or if it was entirely out of time . . .

As it turns out, it's the latter: the explosion is followed by a stillness that Matthias identifies with the silence before the existence of time. We are taken to a place of stillness "As it was . . . in the silence that preceded silence" when "there were neither rights nor hopes nor / sadnesses to speak of," where "in the high and highest places everything was still." We're outside of time, and certainly outside of the totalized, catastrophic history with which the poem has presented. Indeed, inasmuch as we are in some boundless place, we have escaped totality, and encountered the infinite.

Another kind of poet would end things here. Indeed, a properly modernist poet would end things here—gathered into the artifice of eternity (as in "Sailing to Byzantium"), or purged of worldliness by fire (as in "Little Gidding"). But Matthias doesn't. Instead of turning from the world of history, he returns to it—in fact, for the first time in the poem, he enters history by name, appearing with his wife Diana on the pilgrim trails. Here's the passage:

> Towards Pamplona, long long after all Navarre
> was Spain, and after the end
> of the Kingdom of Aragón, & after the end of the end,
>
> I, John, walked with my wife Diana
> down from the Somport Pass following the silence
> that invited and received my song

It goes on, in prose saturated with more proper nouns—twenty-nine in twenty-one lines—to describe John and Diana "blest and besotted" in Spain, and in their moment of history. Escape to a timeless realm would be the Gnostic's happy ending, but the true spiritual tradition informing *A Gathering of Ways* turns out to be something rather different, the best analog for which is the philosophy of Emmanuel Levinas. For Levinas, the encounter with the unbounded or infinite is not an end in itself: rather, it returns us to experience with a sense of wonder, and an invitation to enter into dialogue with the world. And this sort of return and invitation is what we get in "A Compostela Diptych" when Matthias appears in the historical terrain of his poem, and when the silence "invite[s] and receive[s]" his song. The encounter with the infinite releases him from a sense that history is catastrophe and nothing more. Moreover, by inviting Matthias's particular song, the infinite shows it welcomes proliferation, rather than the reductions of totalization: Matthias's song is just one voice in a boundless infinity, not the total summation of all things.

It's important to note the role of proper names here, because it underlines a slight difference between Matthias and Levinas. For Levinas, the encounter with the infinite comes about through confronting a human face, in all its particularity. For Matthias, though, the encounter with the infinite is with something still and silent and beyond us. But the effect of that encounter is to return us to the world of specific people and places, the world of proper names—and to show us that this world is not reducible to some totalized history of catastrophe. Particularity trumps totalization at the end of the poem, as a litany of proper names unassimilated into a grand pattern of catastrophe leaves us blessed and besotted. In the end, it is this return that prevents Matthias from being a Gnostic. As much as he is fascinated with that tradition, he can't join it: he is too much in love with all of us who can be named.

A COMPOSTELA DIPTYCH

by John Matthias

Part I.
FRANCE

I

Via Tolosana, Via Podiensis.
There among the tall and narrow cypresses,
the white sarcophagi of Arles

worn by centuries of wind & sun,
where Charlemagne's lieutenants it was said
lay beside Servilius & Flavius

and coffins drifted down the Rhône
on narrow rafts to be unloaded by St. Victor's monks,
they walked: Via Tolosana.

Via Podiensis: They walked as well from
Burgundy through the Auvergne,
slogged along volcanic downland up into Aubrac

and on through Languedoc to Conques
and gazed into the yellow morning light falling
from above the central axis through

the abbey's lantern tower
and praised St. Foy, and praised as well
with Aimery Picaud their guide

the names of certain travelers
who had long before secured the safety of their way
and also other ways: Via Podiensis,

Via Lemosina, Via Turonensis.
They crossed the Loire at Tours and at Nevers,
walking toward Bordeaux or

from St. Leonard and St. Martial of Limoges
to Périgord and to Chalosse.
At Tours beside the sandy, wide & braided river

they would rest awhile and bathe
or seek the narrow shoals nearby & shallow streams
that ran between. Here St. Martin's

shrine had outfaced Abd-al-Rahman
and they prayed at his basilica remembering
the ninety thousand Moors

beaten back to Córdoba before Almanzor
took the bells of Santiago
for his candlesticks, hung them highly

in his elegant great mosque & upside down.
His singers sang of it.
These walking also sang: Via Lemosina,

Via Turonensis: they sang the way along the ways.
They sang the king: *Charles li reis,*
ad estet en Espaigne . . . Tresqu'en la mer

conquiste la terre altaigne. Trouvères, jongleurs,
langue d'oïl, langue d'oc: of love
& war, the Matamoros & the concubine at Maubergeon.

And there was other song—song sung inwardly
to a percussion of the jangling
manacles and fetters hanging on the branded

heretics who crawled the roads
on hands and knees and slept with lepers under
dark façades of abbeys

& the west portals of cathedrals with their zodiacs.
These also sang: as had
the stern young men, their sheep or cattle

following behind, when up
to high summer pasture they would carry
from the scoria-red waste

a wooden image of their black and chthonic mother
burned in her ascent up out of
smoking Puy-de-Dome (or her descent

from very heaven: Polestar's daughter urging
them to Finisterre . . .
      Whichever way

they came they sang.
Whatever song they sang they came.
Whichever way they came, whatever song they sang,

they sang and walked together on the
common roads: Via Lemosina,
Via Turonensis; Via Tolosana, Via Podiensis.

II

Dorian, Phrygian, Lydian—
modes in diatonic sequence which would order
the response & antiphon at Cluny:

authentic, plagal; plagal and authentic—
hypodorian, hypomixolydian—
Magnificat! Magnificat anima mea Dominum.

And canticles in stone carved in capitals
to honor every mode
in which the honor of this Lady might

be chanted, melismatic even,
graced the choir itself in St. Hugh's hall
where someone wrote the book

sending walkers down the roads to Santiago.
Whose creation Aimery Picaud?
Whose persona Turpin? *The Codex Calixtinus*!

Book that wrought a miracle of power?
or book that answered it and echoed it, reflected
power trans-Pyrenean and uncanny,

causality determined by no human hand?
Did Santiago draw his pilgrims to his shrine,
or did the monks of Cluny push?

Far from the basilica, far from
the *corona* with its hundred lamps & more lighted
there to brighten Pentecost or Easter, far

from the twelve arcades of double pillars,
the goldsmith's workshop & the bearded lutenist beside
the dancing girl celebrating in their frozen

artistry the artistry of monophonic provenance
which answered every gesture
of the vestured celebrant—and far, far before

the carving of a single capital,
the scribbling of a single line of Latin in a single book,
the hammering of gold, the glazing

of an ornament, the singing of the kyrie or gloria,
the censing of the host,
a strange boat arrived off Finisterre . . .

(Or so they say. Or so they said
who made the book.) The boat came from Jerusalem
without a sail, without a rudder,

without oars. It bore his head beside his body
who had caught it when the sword
of Herod dropped it in his open hands.

It bore his two disciples. As they neared
the land beneath the *campus stellae*
where the lord of every geste would heave his

spear into the surf, drawn across the Pyrenees
by virtue of this other who would lie down now
for some eight hundred years—son of Zebedee

and Salomé, brother of St. John, son of Thunder
born into Galicia—
a bridegroom riding to his wedding reined

his horse in, stared a moment at the little boat,
galloped straight into the tranquil sea.
When horse and rider rose, both were covered with

the scallop shells that were his sign, his
awaiting Cluny and his cult
(the carving of the capitals, the canticles in stone,

the singing of the antiphons,
the scribbling of the Latin in his lenten book)
but also *hers*—

Magnificat! Magnificat anima mea Dominum—
who rose up on a scallop shell
to dazzle any bridegroom staring at whatever sea.

So it began. So they said it had begun.
A phase (a phrase (a moment in
the spin of some éphéméride (a change

not even in the modes of music
from the Greek
to the Gregorian . . .

    (And chiefly with an aim to rid the south of Moors, to rid it of the Mozarabic taint in liturgies and chants, to blast the peasant heretics following the Gnostic light of Avila's Priscillian. And then? Then the castigations of

Bernard, the smashings of the Huguenots, the marshals of Napoleon on the mountain trails, the slow dismantling of the abbey for its stone, the twists of floral patterns on the broken columns standing in the ruined granary, the Shell Oil station on the highway through the pass. And at the restaurant by the river in St-Jean-Pied-de-Port (Michelin: 2 stars), good coquilles St. Jacques . . .

III

Aimery Picaud to those who walked:
Beware the Gascons and beware the Basques:
drink only from this well, never

drink from that: these boatmen on that river
will deceive you: trust
only those who ply the other one: and if

you cross the mountains through
the path of Cize, be warned of Ostabat where men
appear with sticks to block your way

and then by force extract an unjust toll:
these men are fierce, the country they inhabit barbarous,
their tongue terrifies the hearts of all who hear:

God they call *Urcia,* bread is *orgui,* wine is *ardum:*
may the rich who profit from their tolls
and fares, the lords above the rivers & the king of Aragón,

Raymonde de Solis and Vivien d'Aigremont,
atone by long and public penitence; may any priest
who pardons them be smitten with anathema:

Depraved they are, perverse and lecherous,
destitute of any good; the men
and women show their private parts to pilgrims,

fornicate with beasts; the men kiss the vulva
of both wife and mule. When a man
comes in a house he whistles like a kite, & when

he lurks behind the rocks or trees
he hoots like an owl or howls like a wolf:
Beware these Gascons & beware these Basques.

But at the gate of Cize rejoice!
From this high peak you gaze down at the western ocean,
at the frontiers of Castile & Aragón & France.

Here with axe and mattock, spade
and other tools Charlemagne's companions built a road
into Galicia: May their souls rest

in peace, and may the souls also of those others
who in times of Aldefonso & Calixtus
worked upon the road and made it safe rest in peace:

André, Roger, Avit, Fortus, Arnault,
Étienne and Pierre, who built the bridge again
over the Mino: for them, eternal peace.

If you cross the Somport Pass
you come to several towns: to Borce first and
then to Canfranc, Jaca, Osturit,

Tiermas of the royal baths, and Monreal.
You will meet the road from Cize
at Puente la Reina. Estella has good bread,

good wine & meat & fish, and all things
there are plentiful. Past Estella flow the waters
of the Ega, sweet and pure, as are

these other rivers I now name: the Cea
by Sahagún, the Esla by Mansilla,
the Torio by León and near the Jewish camp.

If you come by Arles and Les Alyschamps
you will see more tombs of marble
than you would believe carved in Latin dialect

spread before you more than one mile long
& one mile wide. If you come
by Arles you must seek the relics of

St. Genesius and St. Giles.
Between the branches of the Rhône, at Trinquetaille,
stands the marble column where the people

tied St. Genesius and beheaded him.
He caught his head and threw it in the Rhône where
angels bore it to the sea and

on to Cartagena where it rests in glory
& performs great miracles.
Who would fail to kiss the altar of St. Giles?

Who would fail to tell the story of his
pious life? On the golden coffer there behind his
altar in the second register are Aries,

Taurus, Gemini and Cancer with the other signs
winding among golden flowers on a vine.
A crystal trout stands erect there on his tail.

May the Hungarians blush to say they have
his body. May the monks of Chamalières be confounded.
I, Arnauld du Mont, transcribe today

the writings of Picaud, describe the roads the
states the castles towns and mountains
waters wells and fishes men and lands and saints

the habits customs routes and weathers in this
fifth book of the *Codex Calixtinus*
on the stages of the way to Santiago.

IV

From Mont Saint-Michel to Sens,
from Besançon to Finisterre, a darkness fell at noon,
the walls of houses cracked, down

from all the bell towers tumbled bells.
In the encampment, flames leapt from spears of ash & apple,
hauberks buckled, steel casques burst,

bears and leopards walked among the men in Charles' dream
For so he dreamed. Dreamed within
a dream Roland's requiem before the ships

of Baligant sailed up the Ebro,
their mastheads and their prows decked and lighted
through the night with lamps and rubies

in the story that Turaldos tells.
(From Ostabat, the Port of Cize, Val Carlos—then
the high road trod by Gascons & the Basques:

The road below was made by strangers and their armies.
Turonensis, Lemosina, Podiensis:
Straight to Spain each one through Roncevaux.)

They came to him among the Saxons saying:
join us against the Omayyads
at Saragossa: march with us to Abd-al-Rahman's hall.

It was Suleiman himself, governor of Barcelona,
Abbasid and loyal to
the Caliphate of Baghdad. Charles made it a crusade.

Burgundians and Lombards, Goths and Provençals,
Austrasians and Bavarians
loyal to the Reich found themselves conscripted

for the Frankish Blitzkreig. For this was *Hereban:*
this was draft trumpeted by missi
all across Imperium: this was all incumbent on

vicarius and count. And so they came.
They came with sumpter, destrier,
& palfrey; they came with cooks & carpenters & sheep.

They marched away looking like a tribe of nomads
followed by the peddlers & the jugglers,
the singers & the whores. And crossed the mountains

at the Port of Cize. In the Cluny version
there is no Suleiman & no alliance.
Everything is supernatural power. The walls of Pamplona

fall at Charles' approach. He curses
and Luçerna is a great salt lake in which there swims
a single large black bass.

Turpini Historia Karoli: "I am James the son of
Zebedee whom Herod slew. My body
is Galicia. Seek me in this dream & I will be your stay.

My body is Galicia; my soul a field of stars."
Off he marched to Compostela;
At Finisterre he threw his spear into the sea.

In the lives of Einhard and The Stammerer, the facts;
In the *Geste* and *Codex,*
fear and hope and song:—

From Mont Saint-Michel to Sens,
from Besançon to Finisterre, a darkness fell at noon,
the walls of houses cracked, down

from all the bell towers tumbled bells.
In the encampment, flames leapt from spears of ash & apple.
hauberks buckled, steel casques burst,

bears and leopards walked among the men in Charles' dream
For so he dreamed. Dreamed within
a dream Roland's requiem before the ships

of Baligant sailed up the Ebro,
their mastheads and their prows decked and lighted
through the night with lamps and rubies

in the story that Turaldos tells.
(From Ostabat, the Port of Cize, Val Carlos—then
the high road trod by Gascons & the Basques:

The road below was made by strangers and their armies.
Turonensis, Lemosina, Podiensis:
Straight to Spain each one through Roncevaux . . .

Before the Codex made at Cluny, the Capitularies;
before the pseudo-Turpin, Turpin.
And afterwards the song. Afterwards the echoing of Roland's horn.

The nine hundred meters to the Vierge d'Orisson.
The planted crosses like a harbor full of masts.
Afterwards the E.T.A.,

the slogans of the separatists,
Afterwards the sabotaged refinery, the blown-up train.
Afterwards the dawn escape across the pass.

From Mont Saint-Michel to Sens,
from Besançon to Finisterre, a darkness fell at noon,
the walls of houses cracked, down

from all the bell towers tumbled bells.

V

Aoi.
Pax vobiscum, pax domini,
Aoi.
      Ainsi soit il.

And Charles murdered fourteen hundred Saxons
after Roncevaux, cutting off their heads,
when no one would reveal the hiding place of

Widukind, when no one would convert. A northern
paradigm for slaughters in the south?
At the far end of the trail, before there was a trail,

there were tales told: narratives of gnosis
whispered themselves north
to bleed in Roussillon when shepherds saw the

flocks of transmigrating souls walk among their
sheep looking for good company
and habitation . . .
                        Even thus Galicia's Priscillian:

Executed 385 by Evodius, Prefect appointed
by the tyrant Maximus,
at the urging of Ithacius, his fellow Bishop . . .

The soul, then, of its own will doth come to earth,
passing through the seven heavens, and
is sown in the body of this flesh. Or would one rather

say, as did Orosius to St. Augustine: "Worse than
the Manichees!" And the Saint: "Light!
which lies before the gaze of mortal eyes, not only

in those vessels where it shines in its purest state,
but also in admixture to be purified:
smoke & darkness, fire & water & wind . . . its own abode."

Along the Via Tolosana to Toulouse and then beyond
they told the tales: tunics of human flesh,
penitential wandering, sparks hereticated, vestures of decay.

They praised the seal of the mouth,
the seal of the belly and the hand; the demiurge
was author of this world;

among the rocks and trees, among the sheep
& cattle, they acknowledged each
the aeon that was only an apparent body, only born

apparently into the pitch and sulphur of a human shape
to utter human words. The words
they uttered and the tales they told were strange:

. . . when I was once
a horse, I lost my shoe between
the stones & carried on unshod the whole night long.

Cloven to the navel by this wound got of a Moor,
I speak to him alone who goes out
with the dead, the messenger of souls

who saw the lizard run into the ass's skull . . .
The Ram presides above the head,
the Twins behind the loins . . .
                                          Were these voices then

an echo of a field of force counter to
the leys on which the houses of St. James aligned
themselves from north of Arles into Spain?

No Cluniac reform or Romanesque adornment to
the dogma from the rustic prentices of old Priscillian
dead eight hundred years before their time;

no chant in diatonic mode, in good Gregorian, but
diabolic danger here. This
called out for Inquisition and for blood.

Across all Occitania, across the Languedoc
and down the Via Tolosana spread
the news: Béziers was ruined and destroyed,

fifteen thousand fell before the walls & in the town
where mercenaries heard the knights cry out
to conjure holocaust: *kill them all; God will know his own.*

At Bram, Montfort gouged the eyes out, cut
the nose and upper lip off all survivors of his siege,
leaving just one man with just one eye

to lead his friends to Cabaret.
This was orthodox revenge. This was on the orders
of a man called Innocent.

Raymond of Toulouse, driven from his city,
fled to England, then returned
through Spain where troops passed down the Somport Pass

along the Tolosana to link up with his confederates,
the counts of Foix and of Comminges.
The chronicles explain that *everyone began*

to weep and rushed toward Raymond as he entered
through the vaulted gates to kiss
his clothes, his feet, his legs, his hands.

He appeared to them like one arisen from the dead.
At once the population of the town
began to mend the walls that Montfort had torn down.

Knights and burgers, boys and girls, great and small,
hewed and carried stones while troubadours
sang out their mockery of France, of Simon, of his son.

It was not enough. Though Simon died
outside the walls, the French king and Pope Honorius
concluded what the Montforts

and Pope Innocent began. Behind the conquerors
there came Inquisitors; with
the Inquisitors, denunciations, torture and betrayal.

But in the mountains and along the shepherds' paths
leading to and from the Tolosana trail,
the old tales nonetheless were whispered still

far from cities and the seneschals, far from
Bernard Gui, his book & his Dominicans.
The cycle of transhumance led itinerant *perfecti*

there among gavaches as far from their own ostals
as the Ariège is from Morella,
the wide Garonne from Ebro's northern bank & winter camp.

. . . tunics of human flesh,
penitential wandering, sparks hereticated, vestures
of decay . . .

Among the rocks and trees, among the sheep
and cattle, they acknowledged each
the aeon that was only an apparent body, only born

apparently into the pitch & sulphur of a human shape
to utter human words.
And in Galicia, beneath the nave, restless with the centuries,

the east-facing tombs out of all alignment with
the Roman mausoleum & supporting walls
take up proximity below the bones in Santiago's vault

to something holy. The martyred heretic of Trier?
Aoi.
Pax vobiscum, pax domini.

    Aoi. Ainsi soit il.

VI

But was it this that found the floriations
in the columns, found in capitals
the dance that found the music of the cloister & the choir,

the song that found the south for Eleanor of Aquitaine?
Trobar, they said: to find.
To find one's way, one's path, to find the song,

to find the music for the song,
to find through stands of walnut, poplar, chestnut,
through meadows full of buttercups

and orchids, over or beside the banks of many rivers
from above Uzerche to well below
the Lot—Vézère, Corrèze, Couze, Dordogne, Vers—

along the paths of sandstone, rust red & pink,
the way through Limousin, through Périgord, all along
the Via Lemosina to a small road leading to

a castle gate, to find a woman in that place
who finds herself in song,
to find a friend, a fellow singer there or on the road.

Or to the north and west, at Poitiers,
along the Turonensis after
Orléans and Tours, to find before the heaths

of Gascony the pine forests and the *plat pays*
of Poitevins who speak the language
sung by William, Lord of Aquitaine, or the Lemosin

of singers who found comfort who found welcome
at his son's court, his who died
at Santiago, and the court of Eleanor his heir

whose lineage from Charlemagne found Angevin Bordeaux.
They came from Albi and Toulouse,
the town of Cahors and the county of Quercy,

but did they find for her and sing
the *Deus non fecit* of the heretic *perfecti* of Provence
or the light from Eleusis

bathing trail and keep and column in its warmth?
Beneath the limestone cliffs of the Dordogne,
past the verges bright with honeysuckle, thyme and juniper,

quarried stone and timber floated toward the sea
on barges by the dark ores of the *causse,*
while salt, fish, and news of Angevin ambition & desire

came on inland from Bordeaux and from Libourne.
From Hautefort, Ribérek; from
nearby Ventadorn, singers found their way to Poitiers.

The sun rains, they sang: *lo soleils plovil,*
while pilgrims in Rocamadour
climbed toward what they sought, singing without benefit

of trobar ric or trobar clus: *midonz, midonz*
in a dazed vision of the lady there,
hunched & black upon a stick fallen from the sky.

To sing, to pray: to find behind them,
south of Ventedorn, of Hautefort, of Cahors & Toulouse,
alignments in the temple of the sun

at Montségur measuring the solstice, measuring
the equinox, dawn light raining
through the eastern portholes of a ship

riding its great wave, counting down the year,
counting down the years, sign by sign
from Aries to The Fish, not to brighten only that

new morning in Provence but latterly to bend
also onto any path
of any who would follow, singing

at the gates of abbeys or below the castle walls
in any language found
where every song was fond

and yet forbidding, forensic as the night.
Did those who sang, do those who sing,
care at all that at the ending of their song,

as at the start, William of Aquitaine,
son of the troubadour, father of the child
they would hail in Poitiers

kneels crying *midonz* to the stars
but finds in Santiago's tomb not the bones of James
but those of the heretic Priscillian?

I am Arnaut who gathers the wind.
I am Arnaut who hunts the hare with the ox.
I am Arnaut who swims against the tide.

*

Near Excideuil, long long after Aquitaine
was France, after the end
of what was Angevin, and after the end of the end,

two lone walkers slogged along the road
and spoke of vortices
and things to be reborn

after Europe's latest conflagration. Was it spring? Was it 1920? The older of the two, trying to remember after fifty years, could not be sure. It was he who had crept over rafters, peering down at the Dronne, once before. He knew that Aubeterre was to the east, that one could find three keeps outside Mareuil, a pleached arbour at Chalais. He knew the roads in this place. He had walked into Périgord, had seen Narbonne, Cahors, Chalus, and now was once again walking with his friend near Excideuil. In certain ways he much resembled the old finders of song, and sang their songs in his own way and tried to make them new. He called the other one, his friend, Arnaut, though that was not his name, and stopped with him beside a castle wall. He saw above them both, and wrote down in his book, *the wave pattern cut in the stone, spire-top alevel the well curb,* and then heard this other say, the sun shining, the birds singing, *I am afraid of the life after death*. Of a sudden. Out of the calm and clarity of morning.

He stored the loved places in his memory—the roads, the keeps beside the rivers, the arbour at Chalais—and walked in Eleusinian light and through the years to Rimini and Rome, in darkness on to Pisa in another war. And after fifty years, and from the silence of his great old age, he said: *Rucksacked, we walked from Excideuil. When he told me what he feared, he paused, and then he added: "Now, at last, I have shocked him . . ."*

Who was Arnaut to gather the wind?

Intercalation

And who, asked the Doctor Mellifluus, were the Cluniacs to gather all *these* things: *deformis formositas ac formosa deformitas*. A wave pattern cut in the stone would have been enough—would have been, perhaps, too much. But apes and monstrous centaurs? half-men and fighting knights? hunters blowing horns? many bodies under just one head or many heads sprouting from a single body? Who were the Cluniacs to gather round them windy artisans to carve their curiosities, to carve chimeras, onto cloister capitals from St. Hugh's Hall to Santiago so that it became a joy to read the marbles and a plague to read the books. The concupiscence of eyes! For he had deemed as dung whatever shone with beauty. (Dung, too, was music and the talk, *humanus et jocundus,* of the monks, or the song of deeds in poetry. The concupiscence of ears! For he'd have silence, silence, save when he would speak, the great voice shaking his emaciated frame near to dissolution and yet echoing through all of Christendom: *Jihad! Jihad!* He looked upon the mind of Abelard, the body of Queen Eleanor, and did not like them. Man of the north, he gazed upon the south and built the rack on which they'd stretch the men of Langedoc after he'd made widows of the women standing horror-stricken outside Vézelay the day a thousand knights called out for crosses.) Contra Dionysius, the pseudo-Areopagite. Contra Saint-Denis. Contra Grosseteste, contra Bonaventure, and before their time. There was, he thundered, darkness in the light. And light in darkness of the fastness, of the desert, of the cave.

And yet, Abbot Suger sighed, thinking on his Solomon and walking in the hall the saint had called the Workshop of Vulcan, the Synagogue of Satan: *dilectio decoris domus Dei.* . . . *Cross of St. Eloy! Thy chrysolite, thy onyx and thy beryl.* It seemed to him he dwelt in some far region of the mind not entirely on this earth nor yet entirely in the purity of Heaven. . . . When he looked upon such stones. . . . When the sun's rays came flooding through the windows of the choir. For he was servant to the Pater Luminum and to the First Radiance, his son. Their emanations drenched so utterly this mortal world that, beholding them polluted even in the vestures of decay, we should rise—*animae*—by the manual guidance of material lights. The onyx that he contemplated was a light, the chrysolite a light, lights the screen of Charlemagne, the Coupe des Ptolemées, the crystal vase, the chalice of sardonyx, and the burnished ewer. Also every carving in the stones—the capitals, the portal of the west façade—and every stone itself, placed with cunning and with reverence according to the rules of proportion on the other stones, and then proportion too, laws invisible made visible by building—place and order, number, species, kind—these were lanterns shining round him which, he said, *me illuminant.*

But to Citeaux, but to Clairvaux: letters which began *Vestra Sublimitas* (and without irony). Acknowledging intemperance in dress, intemperance in food and drink; acknowledging the horses fit for kings and their expensive, sumptuous liveries; superfluities of every kind, excesses which endangered everything, opening the Royal Abbey to the winds of calumny. . . . He'd move into the smallest cell. He'd walk while others rode. He'd fast. . . . And yet expand the narthex and reconstruct the choir. Enlarge and amplify the nave. Find a quarry near Pontoise in which they'd cut no longer millstones for their livelihood but graceful columns by the grace of God. He'd execute mosaics on the tympanum, elaborate the crenellations. Hire castors for the objects to be bronzed, sculptors from the Cluniacs to carve in columns tall figures on the splayed jambs. Abolish compound piers and redesign triforia. Raise the towers up above the rose making of the rose itself a fulcrum. Repair the lion's tail that supported until recently the collonette. Repair zodiacal reliefs and, in the crypt, the capitals' eight abacus athemia. In the Valley of Chevreuse, he'd hunt himself for twelve tall trees, trunks sufficient in their height for roof-beams of his new west roof and fell them in the woods with his own axe, and offer thanks. Nor would he renounce the light—whatever letters went to Bernard of Clairvaux—the light proportionate unto itself, order mathematical of all diffusion, infinite in volume and activity, lux and lumen both.

And then at Vézelay, Bernard. Sunny Burgundy. The Via Podiensis and the city on the hill. Bishops, statesmen, peasants hungry for some kind of fair, thugs and mercenaries, Louis King of France who ached for glory and beside him Eleanor. Multitudes so many that they flooded all the fields waiting for the prophet from Clairvaux who would command them (Suger quiet under some far tree; Suger strong for peace). At Sens, he had destroyed Abélard. Now he'd widow all the women of the north. Rhetorician of the Holy War, demagogue of the crusade, he stood outside the abbey where the Pentecostal Christ of Gislebertus, *sol invictus* of the entry to the choir, measures time. But then what time was *this*, what year? Sea-green incorruptible beneath his Abbot's shroud, he numbered hours and souls in strict and occult symmetry. Were days measured once again by Kalends, Nones and Ides? Was solstice equinox and equinox the solstice? Did lunar phases intersect the solar year? Who had carved a column with the *lam* and *alif* of the Holy Name and was it *zenith* now or *nadir* in the Latin's Arabic? Many bodies sprouted from his head and many heads from every weaving body. Hautbois and bass bombarde began to play, shawm and chime and rebec as the voices sang *Fauvel* and *Reis Glorios*. From Mont Saint-Michel to Sens, from Besançon to Finisterre, a darkness fell at noon, the walls of houses cracked, down from all the bell towers tumbled bells. In a far encampment, flames leapt from spears of ash and apple, hauberks buckled, steel casques burst, bears and leopards walked among the men in Bernard's dream. For so he dreamed, even as he spoke. Dreamed within a dream Jerusalem's high requiem before the ships of Saladin sailed south from Tyre, their mastheads and their prows decked and lighted through the night with lamps and rubies in the story that the emirs tell. But everything would not be done at once. He saw emblazoned on a calendar suspended in the sky that it would be the year of Grace—but it would be no year of Grace when he awakened from his grave and found the month Brumaire: Those before him in the field walked straight over his indignant ghost and, shouting out obscenities, burned and looted in the abbey, then marched back down Via Podiensis and the Rue St. Jacques into the capital. All of Paris quaked beneath the church of St. Denis and night revealed itself in which the very stars went out as mobs broke in to take the chalices, the vials, the little golden vessels used to serve the wine of the ineffable First Light, and swilled their brandy from those cups, then with clubs and hammers beat them flat. Long lines of priests in vestments led through burning streets a train of mules and of horses laden with patinas, chandeliers and censers from a dozen churches on the Santiago trail, pushed before them carts and wheelbarrows loaded with ciboriums and candlesticks and silver suns. *Merde!* they shouted. *Vanities!* And tore from roofs and crannies sculpted figures wearing crowns to smash their eyes out and their jaws into a stony chorus of eternal silent screams. Relics torn from reliquaries fed the bonfires and the holy dead themselves were disinterred. Bells from Languedoc, from Conques, bells that rang above him there at Vézelay, were melted down for cannon and the cannon dragged along the trails into Spain to blast the columns and the capitals, the arms and legs and heads of kingdom come, into the brain of Goya—Vézelay's splayed Christ upon the door become the victims of the Tres de Mayo, the *deformis formositas ac formosa deformitas* of the twisted and uncanny *Disparates,* the black figures on El Sordo's Quinta walls.

. . . how many years?
The Abbot Suger did not know, but he was Regent.
He set about his work.

Pilgrims set off walking down the Via Podiensis from the
    church of Julien le Pauvre.

Part II.
SPAIN

I

And from the ninety-second year of the Hegira
and from Damascus
and from the lips of Caliph Walid Abulabas:

permission for Tariq ibn-Ziyad to set forth
from Ceuta in his borrowed ships
to see if what was spoken by Tarif ibn-Malik

and his captives of al-Andalus
was true: serene skies, an excellence of weather,
abundant springs and many rivers,

fruit & flowers & perfume as fine as in Cathay,
mines full of precious metals, tall
standing idols of Ionians amidst extraordinary ruins,

and an infidel weak king despised by tribes & peoples
who but waited to be rendered tributary
to the Caliphate and subject to Koranic law.

And then: collapse of the Visigothic armies
at the battle near Sierra de Retín,
knights' bodies tossed into the rising Barbate

and the footmen with their slings & clubs & scythes
falling before Berber scimitars
days before the Qaysite and Yemeni horsemen

under Musa ibn-Nusayr could even cross
from Jabal Musa. Then the hurried crossing of the straight,
the meeting between Musa and Tariq at Talavera,

the occupation of León, Astorga, Saragossa,
and the messenger prostrate before the Caliph in Damascus
saying *Yes! Serene skies, an excellence of weather,*

abundant springs and many rivers, fruit and flowers
and perfume as fine as in Cathay,
mines full of precious metals and, inside this bag

I open for you now, O Caliph,
the severed head of Roderick, king of the Visigoths.
Behold the token of our victory!

Died al-Walid Abulabas in the ninety-sixth year
of the Hegira when, for his troubles,
Musa was condemned by Sulayman to prison & the bastinado

and Tariq ibn-Ziyad disappeared from every chronicle.
But the chronicles themselves go on:
A bad time for Umayyads at home, but every

kind of glory for the jihad in al-Andalus.
Which is why the hungry Umayyad, hunted in the streets
and alleys by the Abbasids, was going there:

the young man hiding in the rushes of Euphrates,
then a silhouetted horseman riding through the desert in the night,
the moon on his shoulder, the pole star in his eye.

Landing north of Málaga, he wrote his laws.
Having *crossed the desert*
& the seas & mastered both the wasteland & the waves,

he came into his kingdom, for he was Abd-al-Rahman
and would rule: *no one*
to be tortured, no one to be crucified or burned,

separated from his children or his wife, or anyone
to be despoiled of his holy objects
if in tribute come the golden dinars & the golden wheat

the flour & the barley heaped in bushels on the wagons
to be weighed, the measures
requisite of vinegar and honey, common musk & oil.

And Abd-al-Rahman rebuilt the mosque in Córdoba.
And the second Abd-al-Rahman
Gathered the philosophers and poets, gathered the musicians

and the concubines and wives. And the Sufi at the gates
called his heart a pasture for gazelles, said
he'd come to Córdoba following the camels of his love.

From the columns left by Rome there sprouted upwards
palm-like in oasis the supports
for Allah's double tier of arches, hemisphere

upon the square, fluted dome upon the vault . . .
When they built the Alcázar &
Madinat al-Zahra, six thousand dressed stones

were called for every day, 11,000 loads of lime & sand.
There were 10,000 workmen, 12,000 mules.
By their kilns and pits, the potters & the tanners,

the armorers and smiths . . . Plane, then, on plane . . .
the surface of each building there
a depth of arabesque, brick and faience overlaid

with geometric pattern & the forms of Kufic & Basmala
lettering interlaced with flowers,
framed by grape vine and acanthus all dissolving

strength & weight & structure in a dazzle of idea:
horror vacui: shifting ordering of order
all unseen, water of icosahedron, air of octahedron

fire of tetrahedron on the simple cube of earth,
living carpet in the grid of pathways behind walls,
sunken flower-beds, myrtle bushes

shading tributaries of the central pool and reflection
of the zones and axes of this world
crossing at the intersection where a Ziryab might play

his lute or al-Ghazal recite . . . And Abd-al-Rahman
built on Abd-al-Rahman's work, &
Abd-al-Rahman brought it to completion . . .

Who could have forseen in these expansive years
the squabbling of *taifas*
and Moorish rulers paying tribute to

Alfonso, Sancho, & Rodrigo Díaz El Campeador?
No one walked along the roads
to cross the Aragón where every route converged upon

a single bridge or sang the tales of El Cid & Charlemagne
slogging through Navarre into Castile.
But it was spring. Spring in Burgundy and spring

in all al-Andalus. In Cluny & in Córdoba they carved
stones and sewed the mint & the marjoram;
silkworms hatched & beans began to shoot and all

the apple & the cherry trees flowered white at once.
Water in the aqueducts was fresh as snow
in mountain streams, & everything it irrigated green.

But when the Sufi heard the flute notes in the air
and his disciple asked him
Master, what is that we hear outside the wall?

he looked up from the pile of sand on which he sat
reading the Koran and said:
It is the voice of someone crying for this world

because he wishes it to live beyond its end.
He cries for things that pass.
Only God remains. The music of the flute

is the song of Satan crying in the desert
for the wells that all run dry,
for the temples & the castles & the caliphates that fall.

II

Via Tolosana, Via Podiensis.
There among the tall and narrow cypresses,
the white sarcophagi of Arles

worn by centuries of wind & sun,
where Charlemagne's lieutenants it was said
lay beside Servilius & Flavius

and coffins drifted down the Rhône
on narrow rafts to be unloaded by St. Victor's monks,
they walked: Via Tolosana.

Via Podiensis: They walked as well from
Burgundy through the Auvergne,
slogged along volcanic downland up into Aubrac

and on through Languedoc to Conques
and gazed into the yellow morning light falling
from above the central axis through

the abbey's lantern tower
and praised St. Foy, and praised as well
with Aimery Picaud their guide

the names of certain travelers
who had long before secured the safety of their way
and also other ways: Via Podiensis,

Via Lemosina, Via Turonensis.
They crossed the Loire at Tours and at Nevers,
walking toward Bordeaux or

from St. Leonard and St. Martial of Limoges
to Périgord and to Chalosse.
At Tours beside the sandy, wide & braided river

they would rest awhile and bathe
or seek the narrow shoals nearby & shallow streams
that ran between. And read: *at the gate of Cize*

Rejoice! (Picaud, again Picaud.) *And from this peak
gaze at all the western ocean,
al the frontiers of Castile & Aragón & France.*

*Here with axe and mattock, spade
and other tools Charlemagne's companions built a road
into Galicia: May their souls rest*

*in peace, and may the souls also of those others
who in times of Aldefonso & Calixtus
worked upon the road and made it safe rest in peace . . .*

*For there were times when all was war.
There was a time, far into the south, when Muhammad's very arm
came to lie and work its magic*

*in the mosque at Córdoba, a time when Ibn Abi Amir
took it from its jewelled box
and shook it like a spear at Santiago,*

*made a Via Dolorosa out of every trail in Galicia
and lit a conflagration
which would burn beyond our cities & beyond his time . . .*

From Mont Saint-Michel to Sens,
from Besançon to Finisterre, a darkness fell at noon,
walls of houses cracked, down

from all the bell towers tumbled bells.
In the encampment, flames leapt from spears of ash & apple
hauberks buckled, steel casques burst,

bears and leopards walked among the men in Picaud's dream,
For so he dreamed. Dreamed within
a dream Roland's requiem before the ships

of Baligant sailed up the Ebro,
their mastheads and their prows decked and lighted
through the night with lamps and rubies

in the story that Turaldos tells.
(From Ostabat, the Port of Cize, Val Carlos—then
the high road trod by Gascons & the Basques:

The road below was made by strangers and their armies.
Turonensis, Lemosina, Podiensis:
Straight to Spain each one through Roncevaux.)

And Almanzor al-Allah razed León
and burned the monasteries at Eslonza, Sahagún;
In Navarre, the king gave up his daughter;

counts became his vassals, one by one. On the road
to Córdoba weeping prisoners trod,
year on year from west of Saragossa. In Compostela,

he left not a stone. In Burgos not more than a promise:
That Almoravids would arise to follow him,
fakirs from the deserts of Sahara: that Yusuf ibn-Tashfin

would land in Algeciras, holy & appalling & austere.
His face entirely covered with a veil,
eating only bread and camel's flesh and honey,

he'd annihilate the armies of Alfonso at Sagrajas.
Widows and their children
would go begging on the ashen empty trails

and from Algeciras to the March,
from Marchlands to Finisterre, the dark would fall at noon,
the walls of houses crack, down

from all the bell towers tumble bells.

III

I commend my soul to God, and my remains,
If I be slain by Moors,
to Oña, to whose altar I bequeath

1,600 maravedis, three of my best horses,
two mules, my clothing with the
robes of ciclatoun & my three purple cloaks,

and also two silver goblets. If my vassals
do not bring my body back,
hold them in dishonor, treat them even

as the vassals who had murdered their own lord.
He was ransomed, Count Gonzalo Salvadorez,
and returning—but indeed to Oña to be buried there . . .

And Ramiro of Navarre was returning—
in an oaken coffin to the church of Saint Maria . . .
And the men of Logroño to Logroño,

the men of Pamplona to Pamplona . . .
and the open crypts at Jaca and Sangüesa and at Yesa,
the sepulchers of monasteries on the Ebro,

graves in the churchyards on the Oca and the Aragón,
all began to fill because again
Alfonso had not summoned Don Rodrigo from his exile.

Tañen las campanas en San Pero a clamor
por Castiella . . . He has left Castile, the poet sang,
And they rang & pealed the bells,

but he had gone: at Bivar the gate was broken
on its hinges, the porch of his house was empty still;
there were no falcons there, & no molted hawks.

The portals of the city had been shut against him.
When he rode up to Burgos flying sixty pennons, he kicked against
the lock, shouted with the strength of sixty heroes

to the people of the city to admit him. But everybody
hid behind his curtained windows.
Alfonso had condemned Rodrigo Díaz, & because of this

Count Gonzalo Salvadorez and Ramiro of Navarre
had died in battle and the king's
beaten army was retreating from the castle at Rueda.

There was worse to come. At Sagrajas, in the south,
as had been foretold.
At Sagrajas, where they beat upon the drums all day.

At Sagrajas, by a tributary of the Guadiana
where Almoravids & the armies of al-Andalus allied themselves
but where Alfonso of Castile & León

failed again to summon Don Rodrigo Díaz from his exile.
Because of that, the Moor could write:
Do thou remember the times of Muhammad Almanzor,

*and bring to thy memory those treaties where
thy fathers offered him the homage even of their daughters,
and sent those virgins for their tribute,*

*even to the far lands of our rule, even into Africa;
Bring this to thy memory before
presuming now to cast thunders against us,*

*before presuming now to menace us, for we have seen
you marching from the castle at Rueda with
the bodies of Gonzalo Salvadorez & Ramiro of Navarre.*

But Alfonso would return the bells of Santiago
to Galicia, and he would boast: *I will
redeem my word, I will preserve my plighted faith—*

*and fall upon thy lands with fire and sword
& drive you back into the sea.
There will be no further messages between us . . .*

*only the clangour of our arms, the neighing
of the war-horse, the blaring
trumpets and the thundering of atambours.*

But riding south without Rodrigo Díaz, he would
soon be riding north—with bodies
of his knights and his confederates, knights & kings

to bury in their lands along the Ebro and the Oca and
the Aragón, where he was riding from Rueda
with the bodies of Gonzalo Salvadorez & Ramiro of Navarre.

Tañen las campanas en San Pero a clamor
por Castiella . . . He has left Castile, the poet sang,
and they rang & pealed the bells,

but he had gone: at Bivar the gate was broken
on its hinges, the porch of his house was empty still;
there were no falcons there, & no molted hawks.

The portals of the city had been shut against him.
When he rode up to Burgos flying sixty pennons, he kicked against
the lock, shouted with the strength of sixty heroes

to the people of the city to admit him. But everybody
hid behind his curtained windows.
Alfonso had condemned Rodrigo Díaz, & because of this

Count Gonzalo Salvadorez and Ramiro of Navarre
had died in battle and the king's
beaten army was retreating from the castle at Rueda . . .

and because of this, the king would be routed
at Sagrajas by the Guadiana,
return with the bodies of his knights & his confederates

to bury near Gonzalo Salvadorez & Ramiro of Navarre.

IV

Oit varones una razón! he shouted
in the dusty square,
echoing the *Hoc Carmen Audite* of certain Joculatores,

Joculatores Domini, who stepped around him
and his eager rabble of an audience
to walk beneath the scaffold of the master of Sangüesa

who would freeze him there forever in the stone
even as he left the town
to sing the wayfarers upon their way

from Yesa on through Burgos to León.
On the portal he disports himself with viol & bow,
and also with the lady in a sexy gown

whose other friend is farting in a well beside a cooper
struggling with his heavy barrel.
But on the trail he was quintessential news, was history itself,

and sang the life of Don Rodrigo while El Cid
yet earned the fame to warrant song.
And aged within his story. And grew so very old

his song became a banner among banners
of reconquest: *Oit varones
una razón*—of reconciliation on the Tagus, it might be,

once the hero halted at El Poyo,
once the heralds brought him followers from Aragón & Monreal,
once Minaya sought Alfonso for him

west in Sahagún, west in Carrión,
toward which they walked who'd gathered in the square
beneath the portal of María la Real.

And when Rodrigo rode to meet his king the villagers
& peasants saw, the singer sang
tanta buena arma, tanto buen cavallo corredor—

splendid weapons, swift horses, capes and cloaks
and furs and everyone
vestidos son de colores, all dressed in colors,

underneath the banners
when he stopped on the Tagus, when he fell upon
his face before Alfonso, when he

took between his teeth the grasses of the field—
las yerbas del campo—and wept
great tears as if he had received a mortal wound

and would be reconciled with the earth itself . . .
as act of faith? Auto de fé?
& near the Tagus once again, Toledo's banners flying

long long beyond him who had come to meet Alfonso
from Valencia & him whose song
became a banner among banners of reconquest?

This *razón* was also sung along the trails, for it was news,
and it was news of conflagration
great as that which burned the northern cities

in the Caliphate: this *razón* was Torquemada's song.
Hoc Carmen Audite.
In conspecto tormentorum . . . (As when Don Rodrigo's daughters

lash and spurs were shown by their own bridegrooms.
When they entered the grove of Corpes
following the two Infantes back to Carrión near Sahagún.

. . . bien lo creades
aquí seredes escarnidas en estos fieros montes.
Oy nos partiremos . . .

And they knew it for a certainty that they
would be tormented,
scourged and shamed and left in that dark place.)

Those abjuring marched with tapers through each town
& wore the sambenito & the yellow robe
embroidered with a black Saint Andrew's cross.

The crier walked before them, crying out
to those who came to watch
the nature of offenses to be punished while

behind them came the paste-board effigies
of those Marranos and Moriscos
who had died of torture, and exhumed bodies

of the heretics dead & buried before Torquemada
reigned at every quemadero:
Hoc Carmen Audite. In conspecto tormentorum . . .

These we order vicars, rectors, chaplains, sacristans
to treat as excommunicated & accursed for
having now incurred the wrath & indignation of Almighty God

& on these rebels & these disobedient
be all the plagues and maledictions which befell upon
king Pharaoh and his host & may

the excommunication pass to all their progeny.
May they be accursed in eating
& in drinking, in waking and in sleeping,

in coming and in going. Accursed be they
in living & in dying & the devil
be at their right hand; may their days be few

and evil, may their substance pass to others,
may their children all be orphans & widows all their wives.
May usurers take all their goods;

May all their prayers be turned to maledictions;
accursed be their bread and wine,
their meat and fish, their fruit & any food they eat;

the houses they inhabit & the raiment that they wear.
Accursed be they unto Satan
and his lords, & these accompany them both night & day . . .

But far from Toledo, on the road to Sahagún & Carrión,
they told the tales: tunics of human flesh,
penitential wandering, sparks hereticated, vestures of decay.

They praised the seal of the mouth,
the seal of the belly and the hand; the demiurge
was author of this world;

among the rocks and trees, among the sheep
& cattle, they acknowledged each
the aeon that was only an apparent body, only born

apparently into the pitch and sulphur of a human shape
to utter human words. And the Jews
hid their secret practices, and the Arabs likewise theirs,

and at the ending of the song, as at the very start,
Don Rodrigo asked his king,
earning thus his exile: *Did you kill your brother?*

Did you collude & commit incest with your sister?
For if you did, all your schemes will fail,
even though I lie prostrate before you eating grass . . .

Take this oath upon the iron bolt, upon the crossbow.
Otherwise, may peasants murder you—
Villanos te maten, rey; villanos, que no hidalgos;

even though I lie prostrate before you eating grass . . .

*

When the singer reached the bridge at Puente la Reina
with the pilgrims who had followed him
for some six hundred years, they met an army:

Soult and Ney & other marshals of Napoleon crossing
into Spain through Roncevaux
and trailing all the engines of their empire . . .

... bien lo creades
aquí seredes escarnidas en estos fieros montes.
Oy nos partiremos ...

Aoi.
Oit varones una razón.
Aoi.

    Hoc Carmen Audite.

V

Soult was at Saldaña on the Carrión
when General Stewart's aide-de-camp walked into Rueda
past the cow-dung fires of peasants

to discover there some eighty horsemen who belonged,
he ascertained, to a division of
Franceski's cavalry. These the light dragoons surrounded

after midnight. General Moore advanced from Salamanca
through Alaejos to Valladolid, & a stolen
sabretache with full intelligence in Marshal Berthier's dispatch

revealed that Junot's infantry had yet to cross the Ebro
and that Ney was still engaged at Saragossa.
On forced march, the British trod December's icy roads

from Toro to Mayorga south of Sahagún.
What pilgrims they became!
Everyone a step-child to some devotee of Sol Invictus,

god of legionaries in whatever expeditionary war,
they billeted beneath the frieze
of Saint María del Camino with its bulls' heads

on abutments of the inner arch, racing horsemen,
and a naked rider on a lion.
They'd drag like Mithra in a week their burdens

down unholy trails and over mountains to the cave
that was Coruña. Exactly where the spears
of Charlemagne's unburied dead had sprouted leaves

along the Cea at the edge of Sahagún, they halted
their advance. By Alfonso's grave,
by the graves of Doña Berta & Constanza, his French queens,

by the ruins of the abbey that had rivaled Cluny
built by Jaca's Englishman
where Aimery Picaud had found unrivalled natural beauty

and a city radiant with grace,
these Englishmen of Sir John Moore's found news:
that Bonaparte himself had crossed the Duoro

and would crush them where they were or drive them
to the sea. They turned and fled;
joined a procession of the living and the dead.

Before them, taurophorus, Mithra dragged the bull,
took its hooves upon his shoulders,
pulling it up mountain trails after Villafranca

in the sleet and snow. Behind them, in his death,
embalmed Rodrigo—tied to beams
that braced him in his saddle, dressed for combat,

sword in hand, looking like some exhumed agent
of the Holy Office driving
heretics to new trans-Cantabrian quemaderos . . .

. . . *tantas lanças premer e alçar,*
tanta adágara foradar e passar . . . tanta loriga
falssar e desmanchar, tantos pendones

salir vermejos en sangre . . . lances, bucklers,
coats of mail broken there,
pennons of the foreign legions soaked in blood . . .

If Suero de Quiñones read aloud the twenty-two
conditions of the tournament
in which he'd win his ransom at the Orbiego bridge

and then proclaim the Paso Honroso,
who would answer for these blood-shod infantry between
Bembibre and the Cua not *Oit Varones* . . .

but *Ahora sueña la razón?*
If reason drempt on this retreat, then so did song.
It slept and dreamed its monsters

in the language of a soldiery that spat and swore
cursing all the bridges
that would measure honor & had measured piety before.

No one shouted *Vivan los Ingleses* as they passed
through villages to loot & rape
where church bells rang when they had gone to summon Soult.

Stragglers broke into bodegas, smashed the wine casks,
then cut up the dying mules & bullocks
by the roadside that had pulled artillery & ammunition vans

to boil them in kettles on great fires they built with gun butts
and mix with what remained of issue brandy,
salted meats and biscuits and the buckets full of melted snow.

Those who dared to sleep were frozen dead by morning,
and when chasseurs came in twos & threes
to scout the strength of Moore's rear guard, they hacked

the arms off those who staggered in the wind
or split their heads down to their chins with sabers flashing
in the sun. All the rest was in the hills.

From Villafranca to Nogales, from
Nogales on through Lugo to Betanzos, darkness fell at noon,
the walls of houses cracked, down

from all the bell towers tumbled bells.
On the march, flames leapt from spears of ash & apple,
hauberks buckled, steel casques burst,

bears and leopards walked among the men
in John Moore's dream. For so he dreamed. Dreamed
within a dream his own high requiem before

the English ships sailed north from Vigo,
their mastheads and their prows decked and lighted
through the night with lamps and rubies

in the story that Trafalgar tells.
Miles, Corax, Heliodromus, Pater of the bas-reliefs,
he signed the zodiac of Mithra's solstice

and hallucinated Corybantes in the skins of beasts
and flagellants where General Paget
sought to make example of deserters and had lashed

at stunted icy trees men who'd
hidden in the windowless dark huts with sick & filthy
mountaineers and who, blinded by the days

of snow, could only hear what would accompany
their punishment: a jangling
of the manacles and fetters hanging on the branded

criminals who crawled the road before them
on their hands and knees and slept
with lepers under dark façades of abbeys, while

in Bonaparte's Madrid, El Sordo painted bulls.
Bulls and bodies of the slain—
dismembered and hung up on trees like ornaments:

arms and legs, heads with genitals stuffed
in their mouths, torsos
cut off at the waist and neck and shoulders.

These the *deformis formositas ac formosa deformitas*
of the hour—torsos and toros,
packed in ice, delivered down the trails to Picasso

in a year when internationals once more decamp in Spain . . .
Viva la Muerte's the Falangist song.
Lorca's murdered; Machado & Vallejo promptly die.

Trusting neither Mithra nor St. James, his eye
on anarchists in Barcelona,
Franco summons mercenary Moors to save the church.

VI

In the high places, they could hear the blast.
Ships rocked on the sea,
the houses at Coruña shook on their foundations

when the ammunition stores were blown.
At Santiago, bells that had burned Almanzor's oils
rang from the shock of it while men

whose job it was to ring them stood
amazed out in the square & wondered if this thunder
and the ringing was in time for Vespers

or for Nones or if it was entirely out of time.
The thunder and the ringing echoed
down the trails, back to San Millán, San Juan de la Peña,

while Maragatos looked up from their plows
and Basque shepherds among flocks near Roncevaux
turned their backs on the west & hunched

down under tall protective rocks jutting up
in frosty and transhumant fields.
Then in the high & highest places everything was still.

As it was in the beginning. Before Saint Francis
came down from the hills to Rocaforte,
before he taught his brothers how to preach & sing the word

to their little sister birds who flew into the tallest trees
and over cliffs in threefold
colored and adoring coats; before the Logos

or the Duende moved in Bertsulari singing ancient
fueros of the Basques; before Ignatius
hammered out his disciplines among the mountain rocks

breaking on the igneous of will the *ignis fatuus*
of valleys & the vagaries of love.
As it was in the beginning . . .

        Long before *it is*
and ever shall be under overhanging
rocks at San Juan de la Peña . . . where they say, they *say*

the Grail came to rest and made a fortress
of the monastery there carved beneath a cliff-face roof
where dowsers conjured water out of rock

in Mithra's Visigothic cave & his tauroctonous priest
drove the killing sword, like Manolete,
in the shoulder of the bellowing great beast

to burst its heart & bleed the plants & herbs across
the mountainside that monks would one day
gather there, bleed the wheat they'd make into their bread.

Everything, everything was still. As it was in the beginning
long before the silence of the abbeys,
the silence of the abbots in their solitary prayer,

the silence of the brothers cutting hay & tending sheep
at San Millán of the Cowl,
the silent sacristan measuring and pouring oils—

the weavers and the tailors and the copyists at work,
Cellarius among his stores of wool and flax,
Hortulanus in his garden tending bees—silence broken only

as Hebdomadarius, finished with the cooking, rings a bell
and even old Gonzalo de Berceo looks up happily
from silent pages where his saint has walked the mountains

in the language of Castillian *juglares* which is not,
God knows, the language of the Latin clerks. *Andaba por los montes,
por los fuertes lugares, por las cuestas enhiestas,*

but silently, and all around him it was very very still.
As it was in the beginning before silence,
in the silence that preceded silence, in the stillness

before anything was still, when nothing
made a single sound and singularity was only nothing's
song unsinging . . . aphonia

before a whisper or a breath, aphasia
before injury,
aphelion of outcry without sun . . .

                                      Long before *it is
and ever shall be* under overhanging
rocks at San Juan de la Peña, at San Millán of the Cowl,

at Loyola's Casa-Torre and the shepherds' huts
of Bertsulari in the Pyrenees
when no one spoke of *fueros* or *tristitia* or *spes,*

and there were neither rights nor hopes nor
sadnesses to speak of.
Then in the high and highest places everything was still.

As it was in the beginning. As it will be in the end.

                                        *

Towards Pamplona, long long after all Navarre
was Spain, and after the end
of the Kingdom of Aragón, & after the end of the end,

I, John, walked with my wife Diana
down from the Somport Pass following the silence
that invited and received my song

after Europe's latest referendum. In the city of the *encierro* and the festival of San Fermín, we drank red wines of the Ribera—Baja Montaña, Tierra Estella—hosted by Delgado-Gomez, genius of that place and guide Picaud. From university to citadel to bull ring, from cathedral to the Plaza del Castillo and along the high banks of the Arga, we walked and talked about the road to Santiago, El Cid Campeador, Zumalacárregui and Carlist wars. For he, Delgado-Gomez, was a native of that place. He knew the way to San Juan de la Peña, to Leyre and Olite and Sangüesa—and so we followed him along the river valleys, into hills, and over arid plains in the Bardenas. And after seven days and seven nights remembering the likes of Sancho the Wise and Sancho the Strong, the battle of Navas de Tolosa and the chains of Miramamolín wrapped around a coat of arms, the three of us, blest and besotted, burned by the sun but refreshed by all the waters of the mountain streams, the shade of many cloisters, and the breezes of the vineyards of Mañeru, crossed the Puente la Reina ourselves, and walked that trail leading to the sea at Finisterre.

And, in the high & highest places, everything was still.

Epilogue to a Cycle of Poems on the Pilgrim Routes to Santiago de Compostela

And this is for another, who,
in the middle of the map I've tried to draw, the making,
struggled to a Compostela of her own

in pain & torment. *What did I do wrong?* she asked.
*What did I do wrong
to suffer this?*—The primal, secret, terrified & universal

query of the sick. She did nothing wrong.
And yet she walked in chains
along a Lemosina or a Tolosana Dolorosa

winding through uncertainty & grief
to disappear into unknowable remote far distances.
She walked ahead of me, doubting that

I followed, although I called out loudly & I tried.
But also, when she herself took rest, unable to go on,
at hospital and hospice on the way, then

I learned to wait, a patient too, without impatience.
Perhaps we'd see pass by every single other living soul!
The routes were arduous, each one,

and cemeteries in the churchyards far outnumberd
monuments recording cures miraculous
achieved along the way. You had to get there somehow.

You had to show the saint your poor
tormented frail human body. You had to drag it there
driven by your guilt or your desire.

The journey's so entirely strange I cannot fathom it.
And yet this map, this prayer:
That she will somehow get to Compostela,

take that how you may, & that I will be allowed to follow.
And that Santiago, call him what you like,
Son of Thunder, Good Saint Jacques, The Fisherman,

Or whoever really lies there—
hermit, heretic, shaman healer with no name—
will somehow make us whole.

NOTES

The present printing of "A Compostela Diptych" owes everything to John Peck's willingness to collaborate in the project. Because of his thoroughgoing treatment of the text, I am able to delete some of my own notes to the original publication of the poem in *A Gathering of Ways* (Swallow Press, 1991). That book contains two other long poems, "An East Anglian Diptych" and "Facts from an Apocryphal Midwest." All three poems have been reprinted over the years in various contexts, including my *New Selected Poems* (Salt, 2004) and *Collected Longer Poems* (Shearsman, 2012). Still, I have always hoped that the culminating poem of the trilogy might one day be printed on its own with a full-scale commentary. Ever since John Armstrong published his annotations to my long poem *Trigons* online a few years ago, I have been especially eager to get on with the present book. Much of the "matter" here is not familiar to most readers of contemporary poetry. Peck's scholarship is encyclopedic, his criticism acute, and his sympathy both for pilgrimage and poems-as-pilgrimage almost uncanny in its fellow feeling.

Having written in the first two poems of my original trilogy about places where I felt on very familiar ground—though in two different ways—I turned eventually to a ground with which I was totally unfamiliar, except through the literature to which it had given birth from the troubadours to Walter Starkie and Eleanor Munro. In the summer of 1987 I walked parts of the Via Tolosana over Somport Pass and on through Jaca, San Juan de la Peña,

Leyre, Sanguesa, Pamplona, Puente la Reina, Estella, Logroño, Nájera, Santo Domingo de la Calzada, and Burgos, crossing back into France through the pass at Roncesvalles. I did not reach Santiago itself, and I do not reach Santiago in the poem. The writing, however, became a pilgrimage in earnest when, without warning, I had first to help another person struggle toward physical and spiritual health, and then, unwell myself, begin a similar journey of my own.

As with the two earlier poems in the trilogy, I have more debts than I can possibly acknowledge. Stylistically, David Jones is a welcome and benevolent presence. Indeed his good help and hope have actually become, in a sense, one of the subjects of the poem. The same could be said of Ezra Pound up through the walk from Excidieul. I have leaned heavily on a number of translations. Although the poet knows the various languages which he must sometimes quote all too imperfectly himself, the poem's polylingual texture is essential: it is necessary for the reader to try and hear the Latin, French, Spanish, and Provençal words as best he can. I need particularly to acknowledge W. S. Merwin's translation of the *Poema del Cid*, Robert Harrison's and Dorothy L. Sayers's translations of the *Chanson de Roland*, and the three translations, one into French and two into English, of the Pilgrim's Guide attributed to Aimery Picaud from the *Codex Calixtinus* listed below with my full range of sources. (William Melczer's magisterial *The Pilgrim's Guide to Santiago de Compostela* [Italica Press, 1993] was unfortunately not yet available.) Walter Starkie's *The Road to Santiago*, Roman Menéndez Pidal's *The Cid and His*

Spain, and Eleanor Munro's *On Glory Roads* have been my constant companions. (Much in part I derives from Munro's interpretation of the visual setting and internal structures of pilgrimage in light of archaeo- and ethno-astronomical theory.) Occasional phrases from these books turn up in the poem itself, as also from the texts by Meyer Shapiro, Erwin Panofsky, Umberto Eco, Jules Michelet, Thomas Carlyle, Desmond Seward, Jacques Lacarriere, Emmanuel Le Roy Ladurie, Henry Chadwick, Alphonsus M. Liguori, Edward Peters, John James, Jan Read, J. A. Condé, Oleg Grabar, Henry Kamen, Christopher Hibbert, Franz Cumont, Henry Sedgwick, Johan Huizinga, Bruno S. James, Edgar Holt, and Adam Nicholson listed below. Borrowings in the poem are usually indicated by italics.

I have always felt it incumbent upon me to list as many sources for my poems as I can remember once they are finished and going into print. But, consistent with the very unscholarly use made of often very scholarly books, I usually give them in a higgledy-piggledy kind of way. Still, I owe almost everything to this odd little library.

Sources for Part I: Jeanne Vielliard, *Guide De Pèlerin de Saint-Jacques de Compostelle* (Texte Latin du XIIe Siècle, Édité et Traduit en Francais d'Apres Les Manuscripts de Compostelle et de Ripoll); Constantine Christofides, *Notes Toward a History of Medieval and Renaissance Art, with a Translation of 'The Pilgrim's Guide to Saint James of Compostela'*; Paula L. Gerson, Annie Shaver Crandall, and M. Alison Stones, eds. and translators, *Pilgrims' Guide to Santiago de Compostela*; A. Kingsley Porter, *Romanesque*

Sculpture of the Pilgrimage Roads; Meyer Shapiro, *Romanesque Art;* Joseph Gantner, *The Glory of Romanesque Art*; Vera Hell, *The Great Pilgrimage of the Middle Ages*; Eusebio Goicoechea Arrondo, *The Way to Santiago*; *El Camino de Santiago: Guia Del Peregrino*; Eleanor Munro, *On Glory Roads: A Pilgrim's Book about Pilgrimage*; Walter Starkie, *The Road to Santiago*; Noreen Hunt, *Cluniac Monasticism in the Central Middle Ages, Cluny under Saint Hugh 1049–1109*; Jacobus de Voragine, *The Golden Legend* (translated and adapted from the Latin by Granger Ryan and Helmut Ripperger); Christopher Page, *Voices and Instruments of the Middle Ages: Instrumental Practice and Songs in France 1100–1300*; Russell Chamberlin, *The Emperor Charlemagne*; Charles Edward Russell, *Charlemagne: First of the Moderns*; Peter Munz, *Life in the Age of Charlemagne*; H. R. Loyn and John Percival, *The Reign of Charlemagne: Documents on Carolingian Government and Administration*; H. W. Garrod and R. B. Mowat, eds., *Einhard's Life of Charlemagne*; Robert Harrison, trans., *The Song of Roland*; Dorothy L. Sayers, trans., *The Song of Roland*; Edward Peters, *Heresy and Authority in Medieval Europe*; Msgr. Leon Cristiani, *Heresies and Heretics*; St. Alphonsus M. Liguori, *The History of Heresies and Their Refutation* (trans. from the Italian by the Rev. John T. Mullock); Henry Chadwick, *Priscillian of Avila*; Jacques Lacarriere, *The Gnostics*; Emmanuel Le Roy Ladurie, *Montaillou: The Promised Land of Error*; Joseph R. Strayer, *The Albigensian Crusades*; Desmond Seward, *Eleanor of Aquitaine: The Mother Queen*; Johan Huizinga, *The Waning of the Middle Ages*; Peter Makin, *Provence and Pound*; Adam Nicholson, *Long Walks in France.*

Sources for "Intercalation": Erwin Panofsky, ed. and trans., *Abbot Suger on the Abbey Church of St.-Denis and Its Art Treasures*; Umberto Eco, *Art and Beauty in the Middle Ages*; Bruno S. James, *Saint Bernard of Clairvaux*; Donald Francis Firebaugh, *St. Bernard's Preaching of the Second Crusade*; Thomas Merton, *The Last of the Fathers*; Henry Adams, *Mont-Saint-Michel and Chartres*; Steven Runciman, *A History of the Crusades*; Odo of Deuil, *De Profectione Ludovici VII in Orientem*; John Hugh Hill and Laurita Lyttleton Hill, *Raymond IV Count of Toulouse*; Jules Michelet, *History of the French Revolution*, vol. 3 (books 14, 15, 16, and 17), trans. by Keith Botsford; Thomas Carlyle, *The French Revolution*; John James, *The Traveller's Key to Medieval France: A Guide to the Sacred Architecture of Medieval France*.

Sources for Part II: J. A. Condé, *History of the Dominion of the Arabs in Spain*; Jan Read, *The Moors in Spain and Portugal*; Oleg Grabar, *The Formation of Islamic Art*; Keith Albarn, Jenny Miall Smith, Stanford Steele, Diana Walker, *The Language of Pattern*; W. S. Merwin, trans., *The Poem of the Cid* (with facing-page Spanish text of the edition of Ramon Menéndez Pidal), *From the Spanish Morning: Translations of Spanish Ballads*; Ramon Menéndez Pidal, *The Cid and His Spain, Poesia Juglaresca y Origenes de las Literaturas Romancias*; Ernest Merimée and S. Griswold Morley, *A History of Spanish Literature*; David William Foster, *The Early Spanish Ballad*; Cecil Roth, *The Spanish Inquisition*; Henry Kamen, *The Spanish Inquisition*; David Gates, *The Spanish Ulcer: A History of the Peninsula War*; Richard Humble, *Napoleon's Peninsular Marshals*; Christopher Hibbert, *Corunna*; W. H. Fitchett, ed.,

Wellington's Men: Some Soldier Autobiographies; C. S. Forester, *The Gun*; Hugh Thomas, *The Spanish Civil War*; Franz Cumont, *The Mysteries of Mithra*; M. J. Vermaseren, *Mithras: The Secret God*; Francisco Goya, *The Complete Etchings, Aquatints and Lithographs*; Eleanor Elsner, *The Romance of the Basque Country and the Pyrenees*; Johannes Jorgensen, *St. Francis of Assisi*; Omer Englebert, *Saint Francis of Assisi*; Henry Dwight Sedgwick, *Ignatius Loyola*; Mary Purcell, *The First Jesuit*; Walter Nigg, *Warriors of God: The Great Religious Orders and Their Founders*; W. S. Porter, *Early Spanish Monasticism*; Edgar Holt, *The Carlist Wars in Spain*.

AGENSAY, AGENGROWNDE, MATTHIAS

A Developmental Line from "East Anglian Poem" (1984)
through "A Compostela Diptych" (1991)
to *Revolutions: A Collaboration* (2017)

by John Peck

I
Repeat after Me

Information has seduced *tout le monde.* The collective formation of memory, however, no longer goes *in,* having abandoned Augustine's vast camps and palaces of recollection for the micro-fields of the wired chip. We grow primitive, or newly primary. Ortega and Benjamin anticipated this turn of ours; Frances Yates and Father Ong have diagrammed the art supplanted. And poets since Yeats have patrolled the shifting perimeters, sending out pickets but also anticipating some possible renaissance of full-field memory. Such a renaissance will rely on an inner discipline, not on some precocious child of the cognitive and neurological matchmakers. An inner discipline, as the defunct arts of memory have shown, constitutes a place, a locus or topos, that mimics topographies immaterially: the inner chip sans silt and sans silicon.

The epilogue poem for John Matthias's "A Compostela Diptych," first printed in *Swimming at Midnight: Selected Shorter Poems* (1995) as a dedication, commences with an offering probably never received, to a relation who has walked off the map. "This is for another, who, / in the middle of the map I've tried to draw, the making, / struggled to a Compostela of her own // in pain and torment." The depth in this knows only longitude: "The journey's so entirely strange I cannot fathom it. / And yet this map, this prayer: / that she will somehow get to Compostela, // take that how you may, & that I will be allowed to follow." *Compos-stela*: a field of stars, a constellation, or indeed many such. Matthias refers to Polestar in the poem, through centuries an ever-supplanted, at times absent factor (his notes acknowledge the help lent him, chiefly in part I of the poem, by Eleanor Munro on the ethno-astronomical grids overlaying the history of pilgrimage in her lively *On Glory Roads*). Nonetheless, and first off, one must credit with full weight Guy Davenport's ringing commendation of the poem, that it is "objective and clear" (jacket copy for *Beltane at Aphelion*, 1995). *Clear* also in ways that legends, military history, geography, and ecclesial matters are just-so—both down-to-earth and long-suffered. Thus, the *making-do* of loyal devotion while enduring separation infuses the venerable, intricate yet clear practices of *making*, a venerable term for composing poems.

What remains "so entirely strange" among these objective facts and practices is the compound mapping of depths (suffered: *under-gone*) among overlays of mapped/recorded singularity upon grids both devout, historically tumultuous, and zodiacal/astronomical, toward outcomes necessarily unsecured. Misery has no map but a lot of territory; and while a map cannot be territory, only it can indicate pars inconnu. Thus the demands of mapping = making = writing about such overlays of territory aim at coming to objective clarity, for only that is *the place*, only that the medicine.

Such immaterial location troubles the sleep of our empiricism, as well it might, for even neurosurgeons, when they successfully remove an epileptic focus from gray matter, may discover that it resituates itself a few weeks later in a new spot. Meanwhile the literal places of our attachment and customary life, counterpunched by a climate that we go on bitching, insistently assert their claims on our attention. Between these levels of scale and places of contest lies the human situation, the site continually written upon, erased, and re-inscribed. In the long view that we both carry out raids upon and repudiate, the ancients likened our attempts to evoke the natural ground of experience to making scrims and curtains veiling that ground with integumenta or cloaklike myths. Then there was revealed ground, the coefficient of natural ground, which supported allegoria, a truth behind or lurking within histories and tales. Such is Pierre Hadot's sketch of what sustained Dante in the fourteenth century. Marvelous in ways not fully digested by us is that those figures were kept dancing over those grounds through Dante's liveliness and force so as to still animate Mandelstam in the twentieth. That transfusion, Dante into Mandelstam, represents what literary modernism produced most keenly, more than a model and less than a resurrection of the dead: for the self-transplanted poet, the volunteer exile, it was neither influence nor inflection but mystical participation ballasted by language.

Just where might all this leave a poet who is alert to it? Wherever *where* is, with growing clarity through his work John Matthias is there, wherever *there* might be. Transatlantic in both sensibility and tenancy, he has dug carefully in actual places. Mandelstam serves him of late as a hyper-place in his inventory (his most recent book is a collaboration with Jean Dibble and Robert Archambeau: *Revolutions*, 2017). The ground he turns over in both places and kindred hyper-places is neither a bland general matter nor a curiosity, but a task—most pertinently the task of listening closely to his own poems. His involvement with his wife Diana Adams's London family has led him, and his readers both English and American, to carry out bridgework in the foreground while also attending to the writer's non-obvious enterprise of grounding himself. His native ground gets reconfigured, while both it and his adopted Britain hang him out over side-drops, odd angles, and adventures in relocation.

The odd angle may even grin through the surface, as in the later title "As Kew as You"—which if one pauses just there, one's eyebrows go up defensively, or maybe one is ready to join in a jest. Or both!—but nonetheless, the skewing of perspectives is an operating procedure in Matthias's world. The snarliest of the Vietnam years he spent in England with his new wife—not in flight, but extending his basis as a writer, sometime-émigré, and scholar-critic. Such skewings of perspective mean enlargement if one keeps both feet on the ground—a ground that seems different because to the fortunately skewed arrival it certainly is.

    The richest such relocation and bending of view comes in Matthias's late fifties and early sixties, with the writing of "Kedging in Time," a "little epic" of enormous interest (prominent naval figures in the Adams, Scott, and Young families—especially Diana's mother Pamela Adams—with Churchill, Erskine Childers, and many others): a layer-cake of narrative elements supplies vantages on naval actions in both World Wars. Pamela Adams's own manuscript, *The Iron Pier,* is one of these; others are Churchill's *Savrola*, John Buchan's *The Thirty-Nine Steps*, and Erskine Childers's *The Riddle of the Sands*. The principals often know each other or share ties; survivor Pamela becomes the heart of the thing; and from the outset Matthias mimics the careful sounding-of-shallows-and-winching-toward-kedge-bites into expository hints and pointers. *Ground*—the shallows or channel zone—is tested for safe passage: the depth *sounded* with an oar, its passage secured by kedging with small anchor and winch. The OF *sonder* backs the English *sounding* of depth with line and lead; in this poem a cumulative probing of hints and allusions parallels this act, initially the writer's then ours.

    Which Matthias enriches by complicating his riddling: he introduces "Mr. Memory" from Hitchcock's film version of *The Thirty-Nine Steps*, invented by Hitchcock only to be bumped off before he could divulge his scoop to the villains. The key to all soundings thus vanishes in the movie, but not in this poem, where he "becomes the most important single figure other than Pamela" (*Kedging* 170). That import is served by a stripped-down, solo pastoral, with Matthias as lone navigator asking, "How do these and other texts function in the poem? As secure holds for the kedge-anchor of my reefed verbal craft" (168). The intervening account of how the poem got started relates how the page of entries near "kedge" in the OED—about ten or so words as listed— spurred the initial bits of writing, some of these surviving into lines that remain in the poem where "its poetics, as it were, is made plain" (168).

> . . . what's the future of the future tense?
> what's propitious in the past? Passing through the present
> kedging's all you're good for
> with a foot of water under you, the tide gone out, the fog so thick
> you can't see lights at Norderney but enter history in spite
> of that by sounding in its shallows with an oar.
> (168)

The modesty of means here floats a keen ambition nonetheless, to enter history . . . by taking its measure in the shallows with sound means: measurement (sounding), using what Odysseus carried on his shoulder inland on Ithaka, until it was mistaken for a winnowing fan. Which we need not apply here, for history's shallows sport riddles enough, namely: the first panel of the poem deals with Pamela Adams (not yet recognizable, being as yet un-kedged) through Churchill, and her captain father, and toy German soldiers, and Childers of *The Thirty-Nine Steps*,

and Edward Young and Diana and Bryan Adams (all
having sailed the Alde):

> Thirty-Nine Among the Sands, His Steps
> or riddle there:
>   who may have sailed the
>   Alde, and out into
> the sea, but still was not the helmsman,
> she was he, the captain's daughter, child too
> of children's strategies on tidal rivers
> where the toy wooden soldiers rose
> in marshmist reeds and tipped their Bismarck
>   helmets
> to the girls, *Achtung!*
>
>   Cousin Erskine had preceded
>   by some leagues
> and even Uncle Win. Sons of Lord Anchises,
> prophesying war, sang
> of arms and men who had come back again
> *by whom the bundled fasces were*
> *restored* . . . (133)

Arma virumque cano . . . . The comeback boys are Trojans hoisting fagots lashed in bundles around the axe handle of state. No oar, that. And she is *not* he—the phrase's sleight of hand swiftly resolves conundrum (*she* was the daughter of *he*, the captain). And the German evolution into fascism, ushered by Mussolini's Roman stick bundles . . . well, a careful sounding of these shallows simply must proceed by stages of throwing the kedge anchor and pulling on it. Until one does that, the haze of self-interfering atmospheres remains mere enchantment, prompting curiosity, yields certain *Aha!* moments but forestalls others. One listens carefully to the overtones of other times sounding in this time: legendary figures, family, epic integumentum. And if one digs a little, the neatly bundled Roman fasces, admired by the authors of the American Constitution, hang on the rostrum of the U.S. House of Representatives as well as the facades of the U.S. Department of Justice and the Capitol. Erskine Childers was shot; John Matthias hears its report coming around his English world, his oar sounding not only those shallows—the present as his host and only collecting point for guesses, kedge tosses, strokes hazarded—but also fitting him with a silent pun: *soundings* resonant around twenty corners, echoes heard with ears not his alone. The bare serial skewings of a kedging sequence, then, model for the skew-angled resonant epyllion which this poem is. Meticulously hazarded movements in space—gauged by dipstick soundings—fold out accordion-pleated into mazy acoustical chambers filled with the other kind of sounding.

    This silent pun on sounding yields the poem's form. Which turns out to be the second major instance in Matthias—after "A Compostela Diptych" nearly ten years earlier—in which he shows himself listening to his own poem. Listening in order to obtain ground, for one thing: submerged ground in the vast and mazy offshore zone of kedging *now*, as earlier in the blast wave from a munitions dump *then* (during the Napoleonic wars, but registered as if felt on the Spanish and French pilgrimage trails). By taking them in reverse chronological order, I am starting with the richer mix of family connections through marriage and proceeding to the more keenly felt stakes in a loss suffered in Matthias's own family. In both poems, roughly a decade apart, the indirect connection with ground he seeks through soundings, explosively in "Compostela" and in winched, angular movements through an historical / personal / legendary little epic in "Kedging in Time." In both poems the patient task of listening to one's own words—thoroughly auditing them—gains him access to an emergent ground otherwise unavailable to most of us most of the time.

But I have jumped us ahead. It is time now to backtrack through exploratory phases of sounding as poetic probing, in the lead among them our good-old deceptively straightforward friend repetition.

II
Come Again

Placed and sited, and seen as the inside-outsider sees it, ground nonetheless looks forward and in rather than backward and out. Such patient alchemy therefore lends itself to neurology; ground inwardly scanned tracks fully with the mapping of energy curves in our neural networks. To paraphrase Eric Kandel's summary of the action-repose cycle that embraces those networks: the 70 millivolt positive charge in action potential (a.p.) versus the resting potential (r.p.) frames the field, with normal speech awareness clocking in at (-) r.p., the teens keening at a packed 1962 Beetles concert marking an (+), and finally Clarence Brown hearing Nadezhda Mandelstam reciting her husband's "Horseshoe Finder" from memory pushing the needle at (+). That extra increment in the third signal is of course wickedly, permissibly subjective; it is useful news to learn that what goes on in this dimension transfers *signals, not information*—for there is nothing wired, hard-wired, or shorted-out in our mental domain, though most people still discuss it with tools issued by Henry Ford rather than Helmholz and Marconi. What Clarence Brown construes as *drift* in Mandelstam's poems—unpredictable but unmistakable clusters of consonant clusters, root stems, and kindred whole words (linked by sound, meaning, or both)—exemplifies a rich signaling system in a given poem, thick with second-order combinations that have more or less capacity to elicit "system interest." The interest thus awakened is at once phonemic and lexical, musical and philological—in one rich tangle, coherent for reasons specific only to that poem—and therefore interested indeed (really *in* there, *between, grooving* with it all). Brown's Mandelstam is but one example, to be sure, but stronger as a showcase instance, I believe, than drifts that might be identified in even Hopkins or Shakespeare. The steadying factor, the keel in all of this, is that these gliding and mounting signals rest at the ground of such perceptions—they are not information but performance; not data are transmitted, but Bergsonian flows or surges with contours and amplitudes.

Ground of this order is primary and inclusive—the still pool and the waves in our conscious and unconscious functioning. And very old stands one of its means, the linked parallelism and repetition of those forms we call early but which now reiterate their elements freshly in fluent counterpoint to the mesmerizing cybernetic tap-dance of zero-one, zero-one. A signal surges, peaks, subsides; the mind's basis is re-signaling rather than specifically informing. What it repeats is never informative, but always ready in the resting state of a nerve cell to open entirely to influx and altered potency. This gradient of charge affects the totality of the nerve cell. Physical chemistry's reduction? If so, then also the magnification of a signal's totality function—the sweep of a Fresnel lens from a lighthouse bucket at night, horizon-wide.

At this juncture, a swift change of scale, to focus on totality, and with it a turn to face a signal of blank scale and perplexing elusiveness. Geoffrey Hartman writes of it, "Late capital has made its way in the world through an apparently pliant responsiveness to local concerns, local values, local practices, local prejudices: it sells its totalities without insisting on totality as an abstraction. . . . Late capitalism's totalizing strategies are, in short, effective to the extent to which they can pass themselves off as a resistance to totality itself" (230–31). Not quite malign coding, or information's diabolism, but a stumper of a phenomenon nonetheless. My invitation to hold in mind the neuronal perspective on wave totality is therefore pitched at countervailing the gross global totality of blatantly sly con men, con gals, and counterfeiters. Robert Archambeau's keenly astute introduction to the reprinting here of "A Compostela Diptych" aptly cites

Emmanuel Levinas on the penetration of contemporary totalities. Before Levinas, George Orwell anticipated Harpham's view, as did David Jones, Matthias's long study, in his Roman poetry and particularly *The Sleeping Lord*. The Roman cliché still holds, acquiring subtlety and acceleration. Even without the Roman comparison, forces remain much the same in their effects on the coherence of place and custom. For that reason, I take two features of the final section of John Matthias's "East Anglian Poem," its echoes of Jones and its symmetrical repetitions of phrase around symmetrical question and answer, to offer good metal against the Roman gladius or short sword. His acknowledgment of Jones itself announces repetition, implying that the way in which he saw what he saw reaffirms a validity. Still other repetitions ring with an undersense of the changes we know and will continue to suffer, knowing by recognizing and meeting historical patterns with penetration.

One function of informed repetition—a signaling pattern with nuances more than a schematic, binary-informed message—is to face off against the ambient info circus by pinging its tuning fork across textures of bland cacophony.

> After the spectral bride at the mouth of the Thames
>
> Did the tethered swans fly above him?
> Did the deer follow behind?
>
> And after the pounding of magic into the swords?

. . . .

> From the hands of the Goddess of
> Death

> The tethered swans flew above him
> And the deer followed behind (*SM* 96–97)

However differential the cultural critic's language, it cannot clarify forms of feeling as such. Poems do that. The feeling addressed by "East Anglian Poem" is contemporary as well as historical, deriving from locality, not from sources alone, for Matthias has lived there intermittently with his family. Just how does such clarified feeling emerge? First through penetrative form, a technique of radical simplification, and then through repetition. David Jones employed litanies, apotropaic charms, and modified refrains, an ancient arsenal whose belatedness is to the point. In Matthias's "The Noble Art of Fence: A Letter" we find this: "I choose, my Lord, / the short and ancient weapons of our land" (*SM* 99). That choice follows suit from David Jones, though not without a nod toward experiments in defamiliarization elaborated by certain Language poets. Since memory rises because it has been challenged, that form of feeling lends itself to questionings of the ground for speaking, then to progressive revisions of the answer—an interrogative texture woven often by Matthias.

    Although he has put repetition to uses remarkably gentle, nothing less than weapons have gone with him in his kit. Not that this points to victory, however. The fourth and fifth sections of "Six for Michael Anania," confess the odds in a grim little ritornello:

> We did not mean property.
> We did not mean money.
>
> We did not mean Pope
> Or the Place de la Grève.
>
> But no more maneuvers.
> All are vowed to death.
>
> Too late. I have done all I can.
> (Section V, "Rosencreutz to Saint-Germain," *SM* 35)

Such writing wields the lance or the parrying sword, precisely and rapidly, however urgent the matter. Neither manager nor magus is *en garde* here, but the enlisted scorekeeper, his urgency Janus-faced toward both prospective action but also retrospective fatigue. And that is true of our own cultural situation both at large and in detail. Quite double, then, the upshot of the exquisite sixth section, which seems pertinent to both collective destiny and metaphysics: "Qualities tend / To perfection. // We may assist" (35).

The weaponlike phrasing from litany could of course serve regressive, complicit, or even canny stances toward a destructive world-process. Avoiding these, Matthias enlists litany as sheer motto, a focal jab: not "one must fall back the better to leap forward," but rather "one must repeat the better to start over."

A sly stitch of this kind marks "Double Sonnet on the Absence of Text: 'Symphony Matis der Maler,' Berlin, 1934:—Metamorphoses." In its short compass this poem repeats four times, all in the first sonnet, Cardinal Albricht's advice to the disheartened painter at the end of the opera (the libretto is Hindemith's own text): the refrain, sprung tight by the tensed bow of the apostle's finger in Grünewald's altarpiece, commands: "*Go forth and make art.*" The equation of the great proto-expressionist painter Mathias Grünewald and the Nazi-fleeing composer is explicit: "He lies among his tools. / *Geh hin und bilde. Geh hin und bilde* / Polyptich as polyphony" (*SM* 36). One detail from the Isenheimer altarpiece's crucifixion panel, of John the Baptist's hand, answers to the skewering questions posed to any commission-based art, any *Gebrauchsmusik* or *Gebrauchskunst:* Which use to serve in such circumstances? (In the second sonnet a foxy Richard Strauss performs for Goebbels.) Only discernment by means of one's compass needle gets one through this age's knotholes.

> *Geh hin und bilde.* For Albricht, Luther
> Or for Muntzer? *Geh hin und bilde.*
> The pointing finger of an evangelic hand
> Outlasts apocalypse" (36).

A dicey quatrain, that. For the Margrave and Cardinal painted by Cranach, for the rebel monk and rolling powerhouse Luther, or for the incendiary monk Muntzer, what application, which use, and for whom? In every sense and with circumspection, what's the use? For Cranach it was perhaps a sell-out to portray Cardinal Albricht, who himself sold indulgences, whereas for Grünewald (in Hindemith's version), there is only one answer: to ply his brush rather than heave a sword in the Peasant War begun by hell-raising apocalyptic Muntzer, who called Luther "Frater Fatted Pig" and died ignominiously in the Peasant Uprising. Thus, hair-raisingly, exeunt Herr und Frau Hindemith.

And thus, too, the high-voltage *index* finger *indicates* a dire tactic, while the libretto, suppressed, goes on the *Index*: painful repetition unspoken but *indicated*. The Peasant Wars of the Reformation, the European catastrophe of the 1940s—both are survived by an artistic *index* pointed at crucifixion, flexed backward by tension, with Saint John's words in Grünewald's painting elided here, only tone or gesture persisting in Mat[th]i[a]s's experiment[s]: only the reiterative, underlining form of the nonverbal act persists. A refrain is made of words, yet just over its verbal horizon it forms a nonsemantic reiterative gesture, using words to get *behind* words. The second sonnet presses toward certain implications of that fact.

> Abandoned, all the words: for what
> They cannot settle will be left alone.
> Leaving us just where, Professor?
> Contemplating cosmogonic harmonies with Kepler.
> In oblivion with courage and acoustics. (36)

The wit at this juncture, with Ma[t]thi[a]s as poet fully in on that wit, has erasure pushing Hindemith into exile and likewise stranding Matthias as elegist. If the libretto must fail at this point, so too must the poem in hand—"us" insuring that fact. However, if the heard sounds of score and poem vanish, harmonics abide. That is, the science of sound both scored and poetic abides, and ethical nerve attends on them both. The phrase "Just where?" though sardonic also opens at the outposts onto the sonics of the unheard, the unperformed. Only enactment has gone into bivouac.

Thus, with our "What's the use?" question rolling up its messy carpet behind us, we get it: undersense, under-meaning, the kind you take when you gotta leave town and you close all your pores *en route*: reduction goes minimalist or zero degree in the interests of enduring effect. The final line speaks for a poetry that turns to face a culture's falsifying complexities and reductions of integrity with penetrative rollbacks and ears cocked. Their acoustical and wordless thrust comes from doing too late all that one can. Or perhaps it comes from the multivalent drum taps struck by prospective hope but also by retrospection in at least two modes (remember this—it will prove useful; or, remember this—it is now beyond your reach).

In one mode repetitions raise their fingers to point in order to underline or undercut; they are deictic. In fact they index things (even prohibit them) by deploying an expressionistic index finger like the crossbow-bolt-like digit on Grünewald's apostle. In another mode they make sounds that only forms can make, forms that are *of* words but not themselves *a* word. When verbal repetitions work in this second, minimal way, they refrain from naming or renaming in order to round off a movement. And perhaps we should not distinguish too hastily here between primitive and sophisticated poetics. Many are the moods at either hour (and the funny moments in Matthias are many). Courage, however, is one of these, late or soon, signed on for the duration while tapping out the rhythms of what can reliably be known or done.

One can see from a lively poem in Matthias's third book, *Crossing*, how elements of repetition and refrain work subtly and playfully: "59 Lines Assembled Quickly Sitting on a Wall Near the Reconstruction of the Lady Juliana's Cell." At moments the variations resemble those of Susan Howe: "to a soul *that // cowde / no letter:* cowde—// could, cloud / no cloud or cold // unknowing . . ." (*SM* 41–42). Such groping both plays at stumbling and hints earnestly at mysticism. The strands of repetition—there may be more than fifteen—occupy more of this poem's texture than comparable strands in the longer poems. I suspect that only in these fifteen or so, however, does repetition acquire an architectonic quality. Their proper herald is the grimly splendid poem on bloody-minded state grandeur from Matthias's second book, *Turns*, "Double Derivation, Association, and Cliché: From *The Great Tournament Roll of Westminster*." Phrases both from the Roll and Matthias himself volley down the seven sections in cascades of refrain, clanging with understatement. One of these he lodges parenthetically in the Roll text, in section II, as if it has conjectural status there, then brings it forth into his own voicing. First, then, the end of that section:

> (Who breaks a spear is worth the prize)
> Who breaks a schylld on shields
> a saylle on sails
> a sclev upon his lady's sleeves;
> who can do skilfully the spleter werke,
> whose spyndylles turn
>
> Power out of parsimony, feasting
> Out of famine, revels out of revelation:—
> Out of slaughter, ceremony
> When the mist lifts over Bosworth.
> When the mist settles on Flodden.
>
> Who breaks a spear is worth the prize. (*SM* 72–73)

Therewith the line's emergence. At the end of section VI, following a casual reference to Henry VII's murder of a rival, the "Power" passage from section II is reversed chiastically, to end on the same laconic refrain:

> Slaughter out of ceremony, famine
> out of feasting, out of power
> parsimony, out of revels
> revelation . . .
>
>   As an axe in the spine can reveal,
>   as an arrow in the eye.
>
> Who breaks a spear is worth the prize. (75)

The refrain itself had folded out of a source text into the poem; then the dizzying reversibility of values in the world of power, in section VI, folds both into and out of the refrain. The very form of sounding here—reiteration together with chiastic or mirror reversal—says a great deal, compactly and wordlessly, about the ways of such a world, inside-out and up-and-down. It does so more movingly than statement might, for reasons that are neither romantic nor surreal, being as old as the ballads and as close at hand as the same pattern in the massively compact fourth section of the poem for Michael Anania, also from *Turns*, on Nostradamus and Henry II (*SM* 34–35). There, tense-changes flicker around the mirror armature which disposes otherwise unaltered elements in chiastic refrains. Prophecy gets repeated simply, or I should say weirdly, by fact, across the transformer of grammar, in a hall of mirrors.

These two poems, longish and very short, establish a limit-case in Matthias's work. At that limit structure and event both get absorbed by refrain and mirrored replication, as if approaching some region of hyper-density. Splendid, laconic, past being surprised by This Worlde, such an architectonic refrain anticipates different moods in later, longer poems—that is to say, it inaugurally issues the compact version of later, more elaborate architectonic soundings. At such a juncture one hears that tapping of the floorboards which a poet drums when he or she is finally underway—quite instinctively, in order to draw echoes from a possible future totality.

III
Of a Kind to Be Caring

For our purposes, that totality emerges first in two poems from Matthias's fifth book, *Northern Summer* of 1984, "A Wind in Rousillon" and the title poem, then finally in "A Compostela Diptych" from *A Gathering of Ways* in 1991. Each in its fashion weighty, these three poems together play for high stakes.

Though the troubadour Riquièr is present in "A Wind in Rousillon," this poem is not distilled from the roads of France in Pound's manner. It sits tight, as Matthias the tourist does, to study three wind patterns as they transit a single Mediterranean zone: the terrible wind of history from Rome through Catholic Christianity through anti-Semitic Vichy and World War II, and the breath of poetry from Riquièr through exiled Antonio Machado, who died there, to Yves Bonnefoy. But the most embracing wind is feminine—the parching African Tramontane to which Matthias assimilates contrary attributes of the ageless Mater Magna in the tenth section's litany. This section would resemble the Litany of Loreto were it not so compact and so anchored in the history which it swiftly condenses. The Lady, herself the wind, comprehends the sibylline ("scattered pages"), the memorious (binding them), the soothing, the poisonous, the seductive, the redeeming: spirit among all its oppositions. This power also represents Matthias's valiant Irish-born hostess, who risked her life to protect Jews, while also standing as "Mother of ostentation, Mother of ordure, // . . . Mother of Jesus, Mother of jackals" (*SM* 127). David Jones's comparable figures do not stand alongside this goddess; each of the six stanzas in the litany invokes a complex feminine aspect only to have it pass through this place, not abiding there (your house is not the tower, your shrine has grown black, the sea god lounges in your chapel). No prayer, this, although it begins by repeating most of Riquièr's line at the end of section VIII ("Mother of charity").

Just what, then, does this litany perform? In collecting and arranging atrocities, cannonades, persecutions, massacres, the gentle and ecstatic breaths of poetry, news flashes, intimacy, pieties mawkish and true, and whiffs of atmosphere, it attempts the ancient bardic task on nonnative ground of anamnesis or full recollection. Notably, the pages scatter even as they are bound. Nonetheless this litany supplies the feeling of closure on the heterogeneous poetries quoted in the poem, wrapping them in even broader tones, abrupt and biting, ironic or gentle, pleading yet sibylline.

This litany performs something so simple that at first probably we miss it. Whereas the action of poetry typically is to register both cruelty and love, both coherences and dispersions or goods and evils, those opposites here serve one ethos, which the litany presents as care, vast but neutral, the care had by the wind for the ground: embracing but sliding, both binding and loosing. The contradictions felt when all reality is loved are in its care. No illusions—yet the whole feminine power comes, and with it the minimally violating rhetoric of litany, when much of the language for care has been worn out (the Lourdes flotsam in section III) or reduced to bones

(*"Nous, les os"*). Not yet in view, the bones of the great horse slaughtered in Mandelstam's tragic, self-erasing ode, "The Horseshoe Finder," which JM will get to after 2015. It is a dour and illuminating stitch to follow out.

Since much of what this caring power must embrace stems from our cruelty, this litany suggests that Matthias's repetitions often aim at the ethos of neutral but penetrating care, which is not charity: the feminine comprehensiveness that goes well beyond maternal protection, indeed pitiless in its receptivity. Yet short of that, too, such litany is a way of avoiding cruelty. For since Matthias responds keenly to the stories and words of the choral dead, he knows what it is to feel not only his own passions turning sharp-edged but also those of others, mutually amplifying their kinds of keenness. The clear-eyed magnanimity of the poem for Sir Thomas Browne, and the damning but quiet choral voice in the plague ditty, "Spokesman to Bailiff," bracket the terrain across which he moves in this way, emerging from a moral tussle resolved by litany on an embracing plane.

To resume, then: the large step taken by "A Wind in Rousillon" has Matthias pouring anamnesis, with literal considerations of place, through the vast, dialectical sieve of neutral care, and that sieve is litany. Which is to say, anamnesis and literal place pass through the other place or topos of feminine breath, a dry but preserving wind. The implications of this step, for the perception of what grounding might be internally for this topos, which is not a place but an impersonal voice, emerge in the somewhat tentative "Northern Summer" and the decisive "Compostela Diptych."

IV
Ne Place to Lay Yair Heed, Ne Sheeld but Wha' Ye Herald

This tentative aspect is of particular interest because biographical frustration, the feeling of ill fit while relocating in Scotland after fifteen Suffolk summers, accompanies an advance in the terms for inner grounding within JM's poetics. His note on "Northern Summer" acknowledges only his dissatisfaction. Literal and psychological habitation, and the discomfort that comes from not finding it at a new site, occupy the poem's foreground. Matthias rummages through the history of the place—Scotland's romantic courtiers, political exiles, miners and entrepreneurs, Pretender-backing lairds, radical theologians, radical economists, and the hoaxing bard Macpherson in full array—in order to get a navigational fix on his perching place. What he experienced as an empirical unsuccess, however, has good *consequences*—one of the poem's main terms—for the nonplace of poetry.

    The threads of repetition and variation through this poem make an intricate pattern which readers may trace as they choose. What matters here is to show how only in poems of this scale do the subtle differentials and driving power of motivic refrains show themselves. The centripetal or inward pull which I noted in "Double Derivation" has in these poems its expansive and architectonic counterpart. The refrain elements in these long poems address one of the furrows opened by Pound's *Cantos*: how to see and feel ground within one's own making while that dimension is fed by the grounds of histories and places—and how to address it without sounding like Pound.

  These two long poems, "Northern Summer" and "A Compostela Diptych," span the decade from 1980 to 1990. In one, Matthias's English roots through marriage undergo a transplanting which he calls "alienating;" in the second he explores the French and Spanish pilgrimage roads to Santiago, ground at first "totally unfamiliar" but which he came to know firsthand as he wrote. This direct acquaintance takes on unanticipated depth of feeling due to illnesss suffered by both Matthias's daughter and himself before the poem was completed. The poem appearing here as "Epilogue" was first intended as a dedication to the Compostela sequence, but was withdrawn at the last moment only to appear for the first time in *Swimming at Midnight* (1995), that book's final item (153) and identified as completing what had appeared four years earlier (the Swallow Press printing of *A Gathering of Ways* in 1991). It began, as a dedication or inaugural should do, "This is for my daughter . . . ." In the *New Selected Poems* of 2004, the poem leads the final section ("From 'A Compostela Diptych'"), with an altered title, the one used here—"Epilogue to a Cycle of Poems on the Pilgrim Routes to Santiago de Compostela." In the present printing, however, the first line reads, "And this is for another." Many poets have had to deal with family estrangements of one kind or another, and Matthias—who has written at least one very well-known poem to his estranged daughter, "Poem for Cynouai"—is even now unsure about what should be said after so long a time—therefore, "another."

Even before that, however, his feeling was evolving. Among the reasons the dedicatory poem or prologue becomes epilogue, one must be that "Compostela" ends with Matthias and his wife reaching trail's end by the sea at Finisterre. On balance for Matthias, the task he has carried as father perforce takes him beyond the ends of the earth, or Finisterre, as anyone knows who has met with such matters. And it is thus, rather than in some arcane sense, that Compostela and its pilgrimage roads become hyper-places.

That synchronistic convergence of life and writing occurs first in "Northern Summer," where Matthias's concern was already curative in a less resolved way. There his effort was to reground poetry as well as potential residence in a realm cleared of winds. "A Wind in Rousillon" arranged the winds of poetry and history; "Northern Summer" becomes a clearinghouse for this process, with personal relocation as its motive. The zone which he clears has already been cleared, of course, by native and imperial doings, leaving an emptiness at which the would-be part-time settler probes. In that emptiness both history and Ossianic pseudo-history move somewhat placelessly. Therefore, the poem's presiding genius is a bird of passage borrowed from Göran Sonnevi in the epigraph, guiding the mind's probes. The winds it flies, which Matthias clears away one by one as he examines castle, mine, Mary Queen of Scots and Bothwell, the Bonnie Prince, Stevenson, Scott, Kirkcaldy, Lord Elcho, Knox, the brothers Adam, Adam Smith, and Macpherson's Ossian, are varieties of either "consequence" or "inconsequence" upon which language may "move," consequently to some point or achievement, often questionable ("Those workmen died / in nailers' dargs to earn a casual footnote," *BA* 103), or fantastically into emptiness.

Stripped away, then, are the sentiment compensatory to the Scottish defeat tradition, its projections of grandeur and grandiosity in the eighteenth and nineteenth centuries, and even the unsentimental abstract theology and social thought which compensate Scottish romance (Knox and Smith). To leave what basis? Even the tender recollection of hearing Stevenson being read aloud to him as a child, triggered by his wife's voice reading R.L.S. to their children, has language sliding without purchase: "Sentiment's transfigured into history, / and history to sentiment" (*BA* 102). The basis or the ground is something beyond the movement of that chiasmus.

Getting there, however, takes some doing, because it is not enough to replace emptiness with habitation and occupation by others, through their own literal groundings. Matthias of course tries; Sonnevi's blackbird, carrying its "inner empty / space" in a "flight of sentimentality through empty space," prompts Matthias, chiastically again, to hope for some way of improving on the situation, but the sober comedy of it all is present from the outset. Setting King Edward's harsh orders for the destruction of the Wemyss seat against tourist-guide vapidities about Wemyss castle, he writes of Edward's passage:

> Language
> moving upon consequence
> Consequence
> upon a language: Flight
> of an heraldic bird
> through space that is inhabited. (*BA* 94)

Aristocratic action as beachhead for a landing? Such is one of poetry's incorrigible dreams, its backroom longings for its own bardic and courtly youth. Yet the heraldry here also offers something else: pattern, system, a secular mandala for unmoored contemporaries on their flight-paths. Again, how might that be in fact?

Matthias repeats and varies phrases from section to section along several lines at once. In section I, tour-book language "threading aimlessly / through sentimental empty space" provokes his wish to "build on" heraldic languages of power and muscled habitation (*BA* 93). When one reaches the chiastic "Language / moving upon inconsequence . . . / through space that is inhabited," that phrasing is built on the twin model of Sonnevi's passage and Matthias's first adaptation of it. Sonnevi's lines are indeed heraldic, generating variants which Matthias moves around like quarterings in a shield-space as he seeks the right combination. In section II, Matthias tries to wrench free of the heraldic pattern ("the flight of Sentiment / is through a space that's occupied" and "the flight of Sentiment / is not / through empty space," *BA* 95–96), but the quarterings will not let him. In section I's chiasmus, "moving upon consequence" stands as one line, while in section III's description of the abandoned mine, a twice-repeated paragraph-line—"The tower's erect upon the hill, but nothing moves" (*BA* 96, 97)—nicely develops that crucial plain verb out of Matthias's variant on Sonnevi's bird. Section III ends by reiterating the line, but in truncated form—"The tower's erect upon the hill"—just after a dash of up-to-date, North Sea—oil movement: "A tanker steams across the bleak horizon" (97). The blackbird's heraldic quarterings remain, as the empty space gets blobbed with its requisite dark smudge.

The filling of empty spaces, by this or that ruling passion, frenzy, avaricious grab, or spiritual impulse, occupies Matthias's survey of his new turf. The catalog both shivers and amuses him. It also swells out beyond the horizon of the many local Pretenders; Hume, Napoleon, Johnson, Goethe "filled the emptiness before their eyes / with what they were" (*BA* 104, repeated on 105). Such projective energies come to possess our humble verb *move*; Knox, Adam, and Kirkcaldy "moving through mental spaces" (102), and Macpherson as he "moved along / the circles of the powerful and into space / occupied by . . ." (104, 105). Such projectors are driven, of course; collective defeat calls on them to invent some "feeling" with which to invest "emptied" space (Macpherson's calling at age nine, at the '45 Rising: 105). The heraldic fit remains exact, for Sonnevi's hole onto empty space and the blackbird's iris or "yellow / ring" around its "inner empty space" pattern Macpherson's paradigmatic attempt to achieve the impossible, as he "squared the widening empty circles" (106).

For our purposes, the apparent question might be, "Is not the empty space of that bird's eye this poem's poetic ground?" While agile and canny theory would affirm that such is the case, still I wonder. For now, let us enjoy the fact that JM's wit becomes all-inclusive, for in section IX he confesses himself a forger, Macphersonly describing what he has not seen. He too takes the infection. Immediately, however, he jokingly cures it by aligning himself with Sonnevi's heraldic bird. In natural fact, birds stand as eminent examples of heraldic patterning, at least for poet-anthropologist-birders like Nathaniel Tarn, to whom I shall turn further on.

In section VI, up against memories of hearing Stevenson or Scott being read to him as a child, Matthias recognizes his own calling—to differentiate his vocation as a poet, a maker, from its dreamy cousins. All of these, including his own, are intriguingly interstitial, bird-beckoned through a gap that calls for projected feeling: "There is a space / I have not learned to fill / somewhere between printed marks and sounds / and I am lost in some way too / among the heather, frightened of the distances / when all I want to do is drift on lang / uage into dream. . . ." (100). This variant on one of his refrains ends by breaking *language* into a Scottish dialect form of *lang* and a beheaded piece of French cloud: linguistic quarterings on the word-shield, marking the backcountry of this poem's disquiet and longing. Later in the section he cites Scott to the effect

    that "laws & manners
    cast a necessary colouring;
    but the bearings, to use heraldic language,
    will remain the same,

>   though the tincture may be different
>   or opposed. . . ."
>   *Bearings . . . tincture . . .*
>   Theft and Dream,
>   flight of an heraldic bird through language
>   and my mother's voice. (*BA* 101)

This panel quarters fantasy and delirium with lineage, that most solid heraldic matter: Stevenson with his Indiana wife hearing, while sick in Samoa, bell sounds in Scotland, and Matthias of Indiana hearing his English wife in Scotland, and remembering his Ohio mother, reading R.L.S. and Scott—that is, spliced lineages and the actual, stable generations, quartered on the fields of symbolic continuity, although dreamily, feverishly.

More than that, however: the patterns of heraldry *move* into the field of language through Scott's puns on bearings and tincture, which distinguish solid, unchanging factors from the shifting ones (on a blazon or escutcheon, orientations and design versus color and number). And that move into language seems inevitable, since Mary, Charles the Pretender, Macpherson, Stevenson, the ambitious Bothwell, and Matthias, too, the guest with his hosts, all come ungrounded. The guest's anxiety and disorientation only accentuate what proves to be a native condition on his adopted ground. Eliot said through his Sweeney, "I gotta use words when I talk to you." Northern Matthias is saying that we gotta space out when we come ungrounded (as more and more of us are doing)—that is, fill it with a pattern of feeling. And that this pattern, alternatively empty and heraldic in the chiastic flip-flop which this poem enacts repeatedly, will suffice. In my own terms, this filled emptiness is the inner ground of poetic speech, the nature of its coherence as a field, topos, or "place." The emptiness which it quarters and colors, or renders stably generative, is not only the negative hollow that haunts this poem and initiates its unsettledness.

Nor, therefore, is the emptiness of the moving bird's eye the only field for ground in this poem. If it were, Matthias's poetics, at least here, would neatly converge with an extrapolation made by both Continental and American literary theorists from Walter Benjamin's Baudelaire to the present. While the bird's eye in Sonnevi's poem is not the blank eye of the camera or the dead eye of the crowd in Benjamin's essays, its central void nearly assimilates it to Benjamin's perspective, which, in Rainier Nägele's words, registers the pervasive modern impact of "an eye without a glance and as such terrifying . . . . One might add that in this motif of Baudelaire's the ground of his poetry is laid bare. At the core of modernity, something happens to the eye" (131–32). That may well be, but such ground is not wholly Matthias's here. His ground shifts between the eye's void and heraldic experiments in re-situation. While those experiments afford him no outcome secure from his irony, they do engage him in attempting a step beyond the Baudelairean impasse.

The attempt at that step is *a form or structure of feeling*, short of an achieved and settled form as convention; I borrow Raymond Williams's indispensable term here. And JM's attempted re-siting of ground for himself, both actually and poetically, brings him up against an uncomfortably similar structure of feeling, that of the Pretenders, sentimental and self-ungrounding. Against them, Matthias distinguishes himself as a would-be inhabitant. The Pretenders' structure of feeling stems, however, from their status as internal and actual exiles, and so their kind of feeling shades easily into the major structure of feeling in a great deal of major twentieth-century literature. Also, the more earnest structure of feeling aimed at by Matthias turns out to be a special case of the exile's. So just where does one come out?

While both structures of feeling aim at regrounding, only the one attempted by Matthias may foster alertness to the elusiveness of any potential regrounding. Matthias's reflectiveness and ironic probes thoroughly distinguish his feeling from that of the Adapters, Adopters, Inventors, and Projectors, rendering the otherwise uncomfortable similarity to them less than crippling. And that margin of difference counts, given certain heroic ventures in modern American poetry at regrounding. The juries are still out on *The Cantos* and *The Maximus Poems* in this regard. "Northern Summer" hardly sets itself up for comparison with those poems, yet it tries on a limited scale to do what Pound left undone and Olson left monumentally revised but incomplete: the disentangling of a reflective movement from a projective one. The heraldic symbolism and structure of storied ground or lived field disengage from most of the projector's impulses; precisely because these can recombine their elements stably, they are pledged not to feeling but to the possibilities of feeling. Matthias's chiastic flip-flops between projected or empty feeling and heraldic structures of feeling constitute his poetic ground in the poem. That alternation is both consciously chosen and comedically suffered.

Poet, anthropologist, translator, and birder Nathaniel Tarn has turned a long furrow in this field, notably in "The Heraldic Vision: A Cognitive Model for Comparative Aesthetics" (1976). Matthias's forays into exploratory second-homing independently approximate the shield-quarterings in Tarn's mapping of the grids for this terrain, notably the rhythms of conflict and reconstitution turned up in the search, and thus the individual stakes wagered in the whole endeavor—in Tarn's phrasing as follows:

> The question of function must be gone into for heraldry in general insofar as there does seem to be a problem in developmental psychology regarding the exact function between function and decoration. . . . Do [two men] fight on meeting because they have swords and shields, or because their shields are of a different color? Such a naïve question reminds us that shields seem to identify individuals before they identify groups and lineages: or is this an illusion? (27)

Tarn's active module for this heraldic field, valid for Blake, Levi-Strauss, and Victor Turner, borrows Turner's process terms: initial totality, detotalization, retotalization (paraphrased by Tarn as ecclesia-sparagmos-ecclesia nova: 29). Matthias's search for new ground both within and without, on a transatlantic basis, installs the search for new totality in a heraldic frame—so that shield quarterings, though they do not correspond to our triad of grounding, clearing of that ground, and regrounding, nonetheless serve those matters. To my own way of understanding these kindred paradigms for development, all frame an aporetic middle passage, an initiatic enlargement of the needle's eye. The late fourteenth-century Chinese doctor and painter-poet Wang Lü put it this way: "Since I lost myself, I had to follow myself" (Liscomb 15)—a handy compass for a man anxiously cobbling together a personal heraldry whose provisional ground embraces woad-blue northern Britain and Hoosier Indiana.

Taking up section IX again, where Matthias catches the Pretender's emptiness-filling infection and then attempts a cure. "Tourist? Paying guest— / of language of / the place, but heading further north and pledging silence" (*BA* 107). The poetic act after all is to fly and to flee, as bird, Bothwell, and Brecht—disgraced Bothwell's route into exile, movingly speculated, is followed by a glimpse of Brecht's to Finland—with Brecht's impish glimpse of "a smallish hidden door" in Lapland, and Matthias's impish pledge of his bird-similar to a Hanseatic taxidermist, which in the dissolving last lines takes its Sonnevian attributes through Brecht's Lapland aperture (109). (Probably we saw it lift off on stubby chiastic wings: "/ of language of /"). Bothwell, like Cumberland in putting down the '45 Rising, was one "through whom the language of the place / spoke itself to consequence" (108). A real and flagrant actor, a liar, killer, ravisher, and cheat, but no sentimentalist. Brecht the sly poet—"No, Senator, I never wrote that poem"—scuttles off to make the space he must make to carry his word: topos with sufficient inner ground to stand on, and a smallish hidden door. The double identity for Matthias here underwrites both heraldic space (in Sonnevi's blackbird, in Bothwell's arrogant successes then flight, in "bearings" for navigation and "tincture" for ethos) and movement upon language into exile (bearings taken anew because of taint or stain). Therefore "Theft and Dream" may include the notorious thief Bothwell, from its survey of dishonored connections between language and ground, the man in flight spanning an immaterial place or topos.

Matthias has this happen by subtly reiterating refrain elements and their variants. He makes petition for one kind of place (not to be had), but through repetition advances on a cure for that loss of literal footing, that cure being chiastic inner ground. The reiterative aspects of poetics, hoary and taken for granted, actually stand closer to the educated layer in culture than we admit that they do, breaking through that layer in moments of disequilibrium and need. One literate homesick man thus gropes for the whole tribe, the gap at his feet representative. The long prayer of anamnesis by the candle-bearer in Jones's "The Sleeping Lord," exfoliated from a microsecond of loving awareness of the dead, stands at this same opening. Matthias's "Northern Summer" stands at another, first folding a long, comedic, unsettled inventory around the refrains squared off Sonnevi's blackbird, and then refolding that inventory into the bird's passage across the poem, in-out, whisht-

whisht, over vanishing ground.

Other poems by Matthias could furnish this comparison, but only this one lays out a kit for surveying its peculiar basis. In that kit are both phenomena and symbols. The phenomena embrace dislocation, search, research, further disorientation, involuntary memory of feeling, demystification of claims put forward by new ground, anxiety, mimicry by con-artists, and self-mocking exits from the tension—with a hint that integrity has been slyly found. The symbols (they are more than themes) whirl through each other: exile, displacement, and flight; movement into and out of language, and into and out of (compromised) action and ground; and finally there come emptiness and habitation. The demystifying impulse in the poem is self-curative, for it sees through the mystiques of both place and action in order to ground the mind more adequately. Matthias's position as an inside-outsider makes that cure no less valuable or necessary.

"Exile plainly *is*," writes Tarn elsewhere, arguing that it best symbolizes the site of poetic voicing as well as many major cross-cultural mythemes (*Views from the Weaving Mountain* 326). His argument might seem invalid only if Augustine's land of unlikeness were also invalid, or the Hebraic poetic tradition all the way through Jabès were unconvincing. Tarn's careful elaboration of a heraldic schema for poetics, both structural and metaphoric, again offers company to Matthias, tugging as it does at the procedure in "Northern Summer."

Augustine was perhaps the first to test this vanishing-and-reappearing ground in flight. His inquest into memory in the *Confessions*, conducted in his love song to the silent God, progresses to this crucial inference:

> Why do I ask in which area of my memory you dwell, as if there really are places there?
>
> Where then did I find you to be able to learn of you . . . if not in the fact that you transcend me? There is no place, whether we go backwards or forwards; there can be no question of place. (200–201)

This pivotal inference, far from winging-it over the void, exerts claims on a release from anxiety and search. Inner ground comes to hand in the immediacy of transcendence. (The passage to which Augustine alludes in Plotinus, on time—the *Enneads* IV.4.10.5—insists on that immediacy: "we must leave out all notions of stage or progress, and recognize one unchanging and timeless life.") Tarn's poststructuralist affirmations are attuned to this string in their own way (with mythical origin and end zoned off from process by the functional transcendence of art), even while they reinstate anxiety over the "place" of poetic speech, "on the loose, at the surface, hanging out on a highly problematic film over an equally problematic abyss" (328).

    Thus too, perhaps, the blackbird's song by way of outrageous Bothwell and sly Brecht. But were the anxiety not to emerge—as indeed it does emerge throughout "Northern Summer"—false grounding would not be seen through or demystified, in which case displacement to an inner grounding, heraldic and comedic in the poem, even dishonorable, could not take place. (*Take place:* there it is, for common usage will not release its grip on this handrail.)

Even oral transmissions of the written—the readings aloud in section VI—call into question just where the poet might be. The flyways for them are not inhabited, and their ground shifts across oceans. The rubbery mutuality of "Theft and Dream" rides with the "heraldic blackbird through language" along with mother's voice. The shift to the oral, and presumably therefore to primary poetic ground, momentarily enlarges personal disorientation, failing to reassure the mind writing. Just where does the mind go once it is propelled from previous imaginative groundings by the winds?

V
Add Essence of Ground, Stir Vigorously for an Aeon

Pilgrimage routes cover ground while uncovering and trudging out purpose. The old challenge from thieves on the highway—"Stand and deliver"—on a pilgrim route is transformed into "Pace out your devotion, prayer, petition," converting ground to a constantly deferred terminal and drawing out the long walk itself (walking, adverted Schopenhauer, is a continually interrupted form of falling) into a continually interrupted practice of kneeling.

To be sure, *grounding* is culturally specific, and also, in the West, wears a philosophical portmanteau of somber hue. The Romantic opening of the furrow that I assigned to Pound earlier, in which one sees or feels one's inner ground coming to hand, Heidegger in 1929 had claimed for reason ("Der Satz vom Grund," "On the Essence of Ground," in *Wegmarken* or *Pathmarks*, which he revised twice). As paths go, this essay is hard going; but if we take *steps* in framing an argument, or *pursue* an argument that *follows consequent* reasoning, the lexical roots in our means, term by term, have already been on the move, *taking time* to secure their *grounds*, grateful yet also probably unaware that the trick we have brought off is due to more than a skillful way with abstractions. How so? Because (the italics are Heidegger's), "*the essence of ground is the transcendental springing forth of grounding, strewn threefold into projection of world, absorption within beings, and ontological grounding of beings*" (132).

    McNeill takes care to preserve the verb *strew* (in tandem with *throw*) in rendering the last twelve paragraphs of the argument, which climax, however, in a one-sentence paragraph free of that fateful accent: "The essence of the finitude of Dasein is, however, unveiled in *transcendence as freedom for ground*." In the first edition another sentence followed: "But freedom has nothing in common with grounding or with ground, just as little as with cause or causation, or any kind of 'substance' or 'making.'" Therefore libertarians and revolutionaries as such need not apply; and more about that crucial *strewing* later.

    Heidegger was not the last Pre-Socratic born in the twentieth century; the Klein-bottle topology of that last quoted sentence is of our time. Among those twelve paragraphs, again: grounding and ground, for all their basis in our living and making, sustain—support—lend footing or basis to—the destinies we work out, all the while that ground has sprung from indeterminacy. "The ground that springs forth in transcending folds back upon freedom itself, and freedom as origin itself becomes 'ground.' *Freedom is the ground of ground*" (134). And that accent supplies the fitting tone of back-reach for our traveler on foot, John Matthias walking portions of the trails aimed at Santiago de Compostela.

The epilogue poem supplied by Matthias to the "Diptych," repositioned twice, retrospectively supplies an endlessly resumed beginning ("And . . .") and an ever-resituated middle, in the third and fourth tercets:

> And this is for another, who,
> in the middle of the map I've tried to draw, the making,
> struggled to a Compostela of her own . . .
>
> . . . She did nothing wrong.
> And yet she walked in chains
> along a Lemosina or a Tolosana Dolorosa
>
> winding through uncertainty & grief
> to disappear into unknowable remote far
>   distances. . . .
>
> The journey's so entirely strange I cannot fathom it.
> And yet this map, this prayer: . . .

The map itself is *the making*— an old by-name for poetry—as the father declares: the mapped pilgrimage route becomes the Boolean poem as hypertext of whole-making or healing. That momentous overlay, therefore, determines two quietly odd touches at the beginning: a start that is already a resumption, and a vanishing point that does not fade, ebbing "into unknowable remote far distances." (Among those last three words, which is the ground-term? Is it the plural noun declared so by grammar? Repeat them after me, three times, and then say.) "In the middle of the map" of writing treks an ever-present ever-vanishing remote-far-distant daughter: in that way only, *there* she is! approachable at last.

Hölderlin argued at the beginning of our epoch that to engage firmly with one's art one must find one's own cultural matter, *das Eigene*. Yet one's own is also foreign, *das Fremde,* to be won and shaped, such as Greek Olympian transcendence in Europe. The features of this doubled step ramify. The foreign is no tourist's haul of tasty, strange morsels, but part of a chiastic reversal (as Andrzej Warminski shows, 23–45). Native and foreign aspects generate each other, in patterns like the reversals and variants that emerge in "Northern Summer." Subtler dimensions also hold, as in the apparently simple elements in the epilogue to "A Compostela Diptych"—paradoxes like those in the *amor de lonh* of the *trobar clus,* this time a distraught father's devotion.

That love, more than transatlantic residence, subtly alienates him. The anthropologist James Redfield draws a kindred inference about our culture's stretching of connections with what is our own.

> A society of such power [modernist, ubiquitous] must inspire anxiety in its members. . . . We are not sure that modernism coheres as a culture should cohere. . . . Our interest in cultural systems may then be interpreted as a search for the sources of cultural coherence, of control. . . . Ethnography, from this point of view, is an effort intellectually to rescue ourselves from our own history. (101)

Hölderlin's prestige in America since WWII draws a bit on that history. And Swift's Gulliver already drew on ethnography, anticipating our secret hankering for a compact system of cultural coherence. What psychologists call grounding in the person depends on this *collective* coherence. Ethnographer Keith Basso simply marks commitment to actual places as the source for moral coherence and flexibility—his example being the Western Apache and their "absorbing cultural form of large and subtle dimensions" (138). The "aimless" threading of event and language over place in "Northern Summer," JM's bird-Bothwell-Brecht fantasy while trying to relocate himself, mirrors a shared cultural morale stretched gossamer-thin among the wind-blown facts.

Among those facts usually occurs a shock or displacement that abides in the mind. Hölderlin's contemporary Wordsworth, losing inner ground though with morale intact, writing in Book VI of *The Prelude*, a decade after an anticlimactic alpine crossing of the Simplon Pass, suddenly drops into the abyssal forces reframing what he had seen. The uprooted man, European revolution and reaction to one side, suddenly meets a vaporous abyss within remembered ground. Cultural upheaval and divided loyalties recede before this *tremendum*. Old ground dissolves into a lasting basis, imaginal shock its midwife.

Strictly, though, this episode surpasses cultural coherence in Redfield's terms. Wordsworth is the prince of multiphase inner regrounding in our poetry, having installed in Book V an apocalyptic dream—the mounted Arab and the world-destroying flood—which is culture's haunted power to last, as the abyssal waking vision in Book VI stays just beyond nature's power to outlast it. Tremendous anxieties get wrapped into both episodes. Yet as in Augustine's realization about placelessness before transcendence, anxiety turns to something else: calmly charged acceptance, and steady elation before the operation of creative power's abyssal "unfathered vapors." Both episodes frame process panoramas of consciousness, supplying inner ground, abyssal and decreative, for the place of poetic speech in a culture that has begun moving toward modernization.

Both episodes step around Wordsworth's own preoccupation with the storehouse of personal memory, re-centering him. Inventorying an unmoored early manhood, he drops first into an apocalyptic dream that had come at Cambridge; and then, recalling a decade-old alpine hike in the Simplon region, he discovers that the scenery of scarps, high forest, and waterfalls suddenly drops away before cosmogonic forests and torrents, a process configuring the deathless—and also figuring forth the mind's own basis. Proust and Baudelaire, in Benjamin's terms, make of consciousness either a zone narrowed to shock or to repeated traumas large and small. Though Wordsworth knew these well, he disengaged from them. That particular pivot, rather than the unfinished *Prelude*, regrounded poetics more broadly than has the *mémoire involuntaire* fueling the parallel later process that grandfathered modern writing.

Startlingly in this regard, Donald Davie charts a comparable regrounding at midlife in a poem reflecting, somewhat as "Northern Summer" does, a chapter of dislocation (Davie had taught at Iowa for one year, then wrote the poem in England: "the source of my poem is Hamlin Garland," 610). The poem borrows its title, "Or, Solitude," from Wordsworth's "Lucy Gray—Or, Solitude," in which that child, gone in a winter storm, is wishfully glimpsed by her mother; Wordsworth's note declares his own wish to channel George Crabbe. Indeed, Crabbe and Wordsworth line up to support Davie's syntactic pole-vault into his last stanza.

> A farm boy lost in the snow
> Rides his good horse, madrone,
> Through Iowan snows for ever
> And is called 'alone'.
>
> Because gone from the land
> Are the boys who knew it best
> Or best expressed it, gone

> To Boston or Out West,
>
> And the breed of the horse madrone,
> With its bronco strain, is strange
> To the broken sod of Iowa
> That used to be its range,
>
> The metaphysicality
> Of poetry, how I need it!
> And yet it was for years
> What I refused to credit.

Syntax was Davie's long study. Here it declares his regrounding in what syntax serves *beyond* particular losses, lonely ventures, or even singular achievement. That is, it draws on grounded essence precisely when breaking off a clause in mid-air while sustaining momentum into self-reappropriation. With it I can set down all the heavy furniture I have been moving in this essay and breathe a little. (One needs to know about this furniture in order to live, and even reposition it from time to time, but only if it also positions us for leaps through gaps like this one.) To draw on Heidegger's title, on the essence of ground, such a move must venture *beyond* logical consecutiveness, for it is rather the *vacating* of the premises, the *scatter* of connection, the *ill-fit* of reinstallation, that supply the grounds for—by clearing the ground toward—a long-postponed regrounding.

Matthias's "Compostela" works out a similarly adventurous terminal pivot or hinge with a munitions blast. The metaphysics countenanced as necessary—

necessary as the right kind of horse would be—has both equine instinct and plowed ground calling for acknowledgment. Davie's poem is akin to Matthias's long-involved encounter with the storied pilgrimage routes, because horse, boy, and prairie configure the solitary concentration prior to breakthrough, which differently moved Matthias to the realignment he felt on the roads to Finisterre. Both poems dramatize a genuine *coming-through*, to borrow Lawrence's phrase: the Webern-like scale of Davie's lyric and the Mahler-like closing adagio in "A Compostela Diptych" show that not scale moves things into alignment, but mass and aim.

  Returning to "Northern Summer" and its heraldic search: as exiles driven forth from naive installations in cultural coherence, we look for rhetorical forms that can house our dispossession. To grow with our need while allowing our ground to shift, we require forms that let the mind digest formerly grounded experience while also looking out for some unforeseeable next phase. One rhetorical device serving that end is the variable refrain. It faces backward toward possessional imagery, or involuntary memory, while through variations it turns to untangle personal from historical feeling and face forward. Apparently recursive, repetitions can also be, in this situation, eminently progressive. The past which tap-taps within them, sometimes gripping them, they also take apart and demystify. The next phase of grounding which they have not reached they tap-rap a way toward, a progression that is more musical than propositional. The position which the mind can hold with their help is paradoxical, simultaneously possessed and wide awake. As such, it condenses Romantic and modernist forms of feeling in deceptively simple ways.

In fact, a possessional state haunts "Northern Summer." Matthias's varying refrains move him through it (as language moving upon the consequence of ungrounding) and serve in part to free him from it. The root of these repetitions in oral poetics Matthias shifts explicitly to the written—an attempt at regrounding the topos of speech—without quite allaying the underlying paradigmatic anxiety and its suppressed groan. For this poem only anticipates a long phase of reconstruction. Which brings us to the poem that achieves this movement decisively.

VI
Starfield Go Boom in the Bye-an'-Bye

"A Compostela Diptych" commences with a catalog of the tributary roads to the great pilgrimage center at Santiago. There was a time, it begins, when cultural morale and the people carrying it could imaginatively contain the ragged yet bold idea of an overarching culture by covering its ground on foot—when cultural morale and inner grounding could be trudged out, even joyously. And everything Western Europe has made and unmade of itself on those grounds is suggested by this whole poem's progression, which gently and persistently moves, again, by way of parallel constructions that nestle within themselves phrases and words variably repeated.

Matthias turned frequently to one source when working on the poem, Eleanor Munro's *Old Glory Roads:*

A Pilgrim's Book on Pilgrimage. "Much in part I derives from Munro's interpretation of the visual setting and internal structures of pilgrimage in light of archaeo- and ethno-astronomical theory" (see notes to "A Compostela Diptych" in this volume). The sky-fields and grounds both walked and imagined were fed by cross-cultural studies.

The gathering place for inner regrounding, which as a reader I might try to detach from actual ground, entrusting it to poetic speech—to which Matthias indeed entrusts it—cannot be emotionally detached from actual ground. Surely that is so for readers who may know parts of this route. By a nice chance in section VI of part I, where Eliot and Pound traipse the domains of Ventadorn and Arnaut Daniel, Matthias encounters a venerable fellow conjurer with winds, although in another spirit: *"I am Arnaut who gathers the wind.... / I am Arnaut who swims against the tide."* The "Diptych" gathers winds past Rousillon, and past Scotland, for a sifting of shared elementals—European, from a link with the East that we have not matched, and a knowledge of the Near East and Africa, however filtered through brutal domination, which long antedates our experiment. Though pilgrimage has faded as an institution, as certain polestars have moved into position only to leave, as a symbolic route to regrounding it may be incomparable.

Pilgrimage, however, was not Matthias's chief object when he began exploring the roads in northwestern Spain, from the Via Tolosana with his wife Diana through Pamplona and Burgos, into France via the pass at Roncesvalles. News of their daughter's crisis and departure reached them not *en route* at that time, but three years later, only then altering his sense of the project. He would have drawn medicine from the earlier walks while fixed in place by the subsequent blow. The remedy had been taken well before the need for it blocked his path, just as for Davie the need for a certain medicine from writing—its metaphysical scope and penetration—had been a fact long before he registered its value and his need. These are not arcane matters, but rather they elucidate laws of the heart. The writer only in retrospect can assess how much has come to the table and been eaten, already and plainly, as if anticipating later reckoning. Such realization is retroactive to the balm, with quietly explosive force, more like satori than sorrow. In this light the Simplon Pass decade-long disclosure for Wordsworth stands as brother to both the Iowa-in-England disclosure for Davie and the trek to Finisterre for Matthias. Going before, they enlighten their bearers only later.

    A refrain is a stopper (from verbs in French and Latin, *refraindre* and *refrangere*). Even the idiomatic protest, "Give me a break!" calls for a halt, asking for clarification or correction. A second sense, from horsemanship, out of Fr. and L. *refrener* and *refrenare*, is to check with the reins. We have a good notion of what stopped Matthias during the writing of "Compostela," but also, with this remarkable coda to the second part, we meet with what blew it wide open—a blast in advance of clearing the family shock and any long-term processing. For one thing, recalling the joyful walks undertaken brought relief, and for another his appropriation of the long-gone munitions blast supplied Matthias with an acoustic broom for sweeping clean many a space and prospect. Taking the Trinitarian doxology, a praise song at the ends of funerals, baptisms, weddings, and special prayers (the Anglican "As it was in the beginning, is now and ever shall be, world without end, Amen") [Sicut erat in principio, et nunc, et semper, et in saecula saeculorum. Amen], Matthias devised a stopper that incorporates this incantation of forever-ness, unstoppable creation. Into it he inserts an encomium to silence, which already had taken priority over the doxological incipit:

> In the high places, they could hear the blast. . . . {*bells rock in their towers through the whole region*}. . . . Then in the high & highest places everything was still. // As it was in the beginning. . . . {*four more tercets*} . . . As it was in the beginning. . . . // long before *it is* / *and ever shall be* under overhanging / rocks at San Juan de la Pena . . . {*three more tercets*}. . . . Everything, everything was still. As it was in the beginning / long before the silence of the abbeys. . . . and even Gonzalo de Berceo {*the first Castilian poet, thirteenth century, reading his own lines, but silently*}, and all around him it was very still. / As it was in the beginning before silence, / in the silence that preceded silence, in the stillness // before anything was still, when nothing / made a single sound and singularity was only nothing's / song unsinging. . . aphonia // before a whisper . . . // // Long before *it is* / and *ever shall be* under overhanging / rocks at San Juan de la Peña, . . . {*then two tercets*}. . . . Then in the high and highest places everything was still // As it was in the beginning. As

it will be in the end. ("A Compostela Diptych" pt. II, sec. VI)

After a section punctuator, two tercets introduce a prose hymn to the joys of those hikes with their host Delgado-Gomez, and produce Matthias entering the poem with his wife, in prose, as pilgrims, not to Santiago but to the ends of the earth.

> Towards Pamplona, long long after all Navarre
> was Spain, and after the end
> of the Kingdom of Aaragon, & after the end of the end,
>
> I, John, walked with my wife Diana
> down from the Somport Pass following the silence
> that invited and received my song
>
> after Europe's latest referendum. . . . we walked and talked about the road to Santiago, El Cid Campeador. . . . The three of us, blest and besotted, burned by the sun but refreshed by all the waters of the mountain streams, the shade of many cloisters, and the breezes of the vineyards of Mañeru, crossed the Puente la Reina ourselves, and walked that trail leading to the sea at Finisterre.
>
> *And, in the high & highest places, everything was still.*
>   (pt. II, sec. VI)

Finisterre, at *the end of the earth:* as for carrying a certain care, and also *as far as one humanly can go*. Regrounding, explosion's best child, *strewing*'s human reach and blast radius (a tip of our hats to Heidegger), can go with both parents now. Strictly scanned, this sensuous breakthrough into renewed carrying capacity draws on the spirit that antedated the shock, revisited so that it too may be carried, in hard-won knowledge, to the very end.

Yet by *now* in the poem's structure, already nested within refrain structures and phrases, it is framed by what embraces both *fons et finis*, by virtue of another refrain, though a literally grounded refrain, wittily this time!— for the first bridge is not of stone, but comes with that leap from verse to prose, which at the same moment accomplishes a leap from the great all-spanning silence to . . . a tallying of votes somewhere on the Continent!

We must pause and take stock, for this high-comedic touch duplicates a high-tragic touch at a previous crossing of the same bridge in part II, nine pages earlier in section IV. Let us walk this matter slowly.

There Don Rodrigo, or El Cid, has rebuked the king for fratricide and incest. With it we meet the poem's first instance of what happens at the final crossing for John and Diana, a scoping of time and place across centuries:

> *Did you collude & commit incest with your sister?*
> *For if you did, all your schemes will fail,*
> *even though I lie prostrate before you eating grass . . .*

> *Take his oath upon the iron bolt, upon the crossbow,*

Otherwise, may peasants murder you—
Villanos te maten, rey; villanos, que no hidalgos;

even though I lie prostrate before you eating grass . . .

*

When the singer reached the bridge at Puente la Reina
with the pilgrims who had followed him
for some six hundred years, they met an army:

Soult and Ney & other marshals of Napoleon crossing
into Spain through Roncevaux . . .

A host of the mostly dead, led by one living. Section IV ends a few lines later with a tight refrain that Matthias makes from a line in a medieval chant from the old epic: "Hoc Carmen Audite" (from the anonymous twelfth-century ur-form of the epic on El Cid, line 17: the Latin version, *Carmen Campidoctoris* or *Poem of the Campeador/Champion*, lines 17–18:

Eia!, letando, populi caterue,
Campidotoris hoc carmen audite!

[Come on, you rag-tag human regiment,
Listen to this poem about the hero!]

The first *campi doctor* drilled troops on the Campus Martius; in the late-Latin *Carmen* he amounts to more than that, yet also moves JM to place the Campeador at the head of a host mostly of the dead during this crossing which parallels JM's own.

What comes into play through this rhyme? Matthias ends section IV with the several uses made of the poem as it developed, becoming "a banner among banners / of reconquest: *Oit varones / una razón—*" (Now hear this! barons, a poem) through the prostrate challenge before King Alfonso.

> This razón was also sung along the trails, for it was news,
> and it was news of conflagration
> great as that which burned the northern cities
>
> In the Caliphate: this *razón* was Torquemada's song.
> *Hoc Carmen Audite.*
> *In conspecto tormentorum* . . . (As when Don
>   Rodrigo's daughters[']
>
> lash and spurs were shown by their own
>   bridegrooms . . . ("A Compostela Diptych" pt.
>   II, sec. IV)

Torquemada's savage campaign is detailed through this section, twenty-one lines of the poem translated fluently by Matthias, and the *Hoc Carmen Audite* is brandished by the Inquisitor as a kind of goad (sacerdotal impressment of art: the higher "*Listen up!*").

The bridge crossing at Puente la Reina ending sectiont IV therefore telescopes this bit of the epic into an extraordinary flourish of JM's medieval-to-revolutionary time travel, the penultimate scoping of history and geography before the Matthiases themselves walk onstage into cleared air. They take their cue from the old court epic; a signal winks along the nerve-run; JM has indeed heard, but what does it all come to?

With the old *Carmen*'s phrase now in your ears as Matthias's refrain-stitch through those six centuries, try the coda to section IV again, beginning with El Cid's rebuke to King Alfonso:

> *Did you collude & commit incest with your sister?*
> *For if you did, all your schemes will fail,*
> *even though I lie prostrate before you eating grass . . .*
>
> *Take his oath upon the iron bolt, upon the crossbow,*
> *Otherwise, may peasants murder you—*
> *Villanos te maten, rey; villanos, que no hidalgos;*
>
> *even though I lie prostrate before you eating grass . . .*

*

When the singer reached the bridge at Puente la Reina
with the pilgrims who had followed him
for some six hundred years, they met an army:

Soult and Ney & other marshals of Napoleon crossing
into Spain through Roncevaux
and trailing all the engines of their empire. . . .

. . . bien lo creades
aqui seredes escarnides en estos fieros montes.
Oy nos partiremos . . .

Aoi.
Oit varones una razón.
Aoi.

Hoc Carmen Audite.

With this startling segue, Matthias drops us back into his outer frame for section IV: in the lines which he quotes, 2714–16, the Infante's cruel departure from code—which called for executing the daughters—condemns them to torture in the wilds by Avengalvon the Moor, with the Infante swiftly decamping. Matthias's coda then construes the function marker in both *El Cid* and *The Song of Roland*—the jongleur's periodic prompting to "Listen up!" or "Now hear this!" to his audience, or perhaps a musical cue to the jongleur himself: "Aoi"—as bound into his own refrain: "now hear this, barons, a poem" with "Aoi . . . Aoi," and "Hoc Carmen Audite." By *his own*, I mean that it emerges here and now as his, John Matthias's, own program: *I am listening to my own poem for its next directive, and I shall soon let you know what it tells me to show you.*

The coda to section IV echoes its opening, but also almost returns to the daughter theme, which stays backstage: as noted, the sisters were not killed on orders from the absconding Infante, but scourged in the desert. Oblique to Matthias's retrospective grief and inevitable self-examination, this bit of the story does not serve him, although no doubt it nourished his fatherly last supper with himself. I include it because I am convinced that it impinged on what Matthias heard his poem saying to him as he framed its explosive-expansive coda—impinged on him only to be declared *askew to* what he could read from his reflections as father on his daughter's flight. After all, if he had no way in which to clarify the mystery—just as he could not read his own destiny in this grisly episode from *El Cid*—then surely neither would his readers. What he could do, however, is what he has done: cross into the zone of timely but unprogrammable detonations and stay with the blast wave, the audition, the deep hearing of inclusive consequence. Attributing it to no one, limiting its effect in no way, listening to one's own poem entire (with Saint James of legend speaking in section IV from the *Turpini Historia Karoli*: "My body / is Galicia. Seek me in this dream & I will be your stay. // My body is Galicia, my soul a field of stars," 161). *Campos stellae*: the vocalized legend had once rustled ground from earth into to the night sky in a great dream, an expansion eventually transposed by Matthias into *what he now hears—id est*, what his poem at last would have him hear and enact, all tension released into primordial stillness prior to stillness. Finally, then, from himself to himself: *Hoc Carmen Audite!*

    None of this is simply given. One *gets* there. The coda initiates us into a reshaped energy field, the poet our guide while still finding his way. If we have remembered his invocation of the jongleur's *Hoc Carmen Audite*, we can go the full mile with him that he is walking and chanting *while listening to his own access to the medium, his own poem.* Of course, he has written it; yet the incantation intervenes from in-side, even to him: a trick of high writing bearing witness to more than tricks. Submit to your poetics, only in that way being freed by the poem per instruction!

    The actual ground now spreads a new basis for going on at all. Composed and cleared, this ground has become a yantra, to borrow Tibet's name for mandalas with cosmic features—which is most apt in this case: yantras aim at shielding while transforming inner terrain. Consisting of a burial ground along the outer rim, and the yantra-maker's gods and his sanctum inside, the whole is constructed for individual meditation. Carl Jung's discovery beginning in the 1930s was that Westerners spontaneously produced similar radial patterns on their own. The yantra's corpse field in JM's case would be that string of battles preceding the discontinuity-inducing blast. Real battles, and an actual munitions blast modeling for this poetic one—which his retrospective position in the writing lets Matthias seem to be lending it ear, following the long fade.

    The *ficèle* toward getting us there with him is repeated cueing: the medieval jongleur's refrain on *Audite*, which is cued toward us but also—and this is the art's topknot—it cues Matthias too. More precisely: what he at last hears in the poem we too then learn to hear. Those singers at court regularly nudged audiences as they worked the feast halls, stitching these signals into the score for the tooth-picking wine-bibbing nobles. JM has highlighted the gesture, though, for his own reasons—that is, for his own poem's aims now, not as a historical curiosity out of *El Cid*.

    To be sure, Matthias treats us gently before blowing a hole in his poem onto another field: *that* unexpected measure cuts off his shift into the Napoleonic peninsular wars—Marshal Soult's chase of General Moore toward Coruña—before it can get well underway. This abruptness changes the game entirely. The bloody hustle of military history, tragic epic, and personal sorrow are thrust aside by sheer spaciousness. A ground yonder—or within, pushing through—crests and breaks, spreading wrap-around, attaining the *silence before silence*. (Its elder cousin is the yantra's central palace whose four gates are mined with thunderbolts.) Both his coda and the painted yantras do not lie flat on the page; each is a 3-D or 4-D inner-cosmic instrument. *Aoi. Aoi!* Harken to the poem clearing itself.

JM's refrains deployed throughout the earlier poems mount here to this singularity—in the body of his work unparalleled, and as a construction moving in direct proportion to its seeming impersonality. With it a death practice intervenes in the couple's walks on those pilgrim routes already walked in innocence years before. It is the belated royal flush dealt to Wordsworth long after his Simplon Pass hike, but with trimmings. Not only a breaking-through, but a breaking apart into largeness and depth. Peace to Heidegger, but yes, here, for JM and DM in performance as in conception: it is strewing as homing, and homing as dying into fullness of life.

Something else may have landed in the poem from this profound strewing without Matthias quite intending it, a bonus pitched in *sous la table:* such things also do have a way of happening when the writer has already been managing high stakes well. If it looks more than accidental, then it will specify Guy Davenport's estimate of *objective and clear*. So let us see. *Oit varones una razón!* Lend your ears, gentles.

Section IV ends with that segue from *El Cid* with the champion cursing cruel King Alfonso (*may peasants murder you*)

even though I lie prostrate before you eating grass . . .

*

When the singer reached the bridge at Puente la Reina
with the pilgrims who had followed him
for some six hundred years, they met an army:

Soult and Ney and other marshals of Napoleon . . .

Section VI closes the final bit of revamped doxology, issuing first into the two tercets of introit ("I, John, walked with my wife Diana / Down from the Somport Pass following the silence / that invited and received my song") into the prose that celebrates the blessed walks the Matthiases enjoyed with their guide Picaud:

Then in the high and highest places everything was still.

As it was in the beginning. As it will be in the end.

*

Towards Pamplona, long long after all Navarre
was Spain, and after the end
of the Kingdom of Aragón, & after the end of the end,

> I, John, walked. . . .

The prose portion of the coda, some fourteen lines, caps the itinerary with a six-line sentence, ending: "And after seven days and seven nights . . . the three of us . . .

> crossed the Puente la Reina ourselves, and walked that trail leading to the sea at Finisterre.
>
> *And, in the high & highest places, everything was still.*

It is that resonant "ourselves" which sends the ear back for a necessary precedent, which waits in only one place, at our crossing into the coda for section IV: "When the singer reached the bridge at Puente la Reina. . . ." The two poets listening attentively to their own poems are the anonymous Spanish master and Matthias. Both transit points, at the ends of IV and V, are given asterisks to set off the initial coda in IV and the final coda in V. At the end of IV, *Aoi* joins *Oit varones* and *Hoc Carmen Audite*—to inaugurate V, bringing on the French under Soult, harrying Moore—"What pilgrims they became!"—and a conflation of this pursuit with figures of Mithras and the bull on a cathedral frieze, and King Alfonso's grave, and Rodrigo propped in his saddle, from *El Cid*: the final panel in this phantasmagoria features the inevitable; "Franco summons mercenary Moors to save the church." A cavalcade of six hundred years, as announced, inflects into the mysterious munitions blast.

The two asterisks I have mentioned punctuate endings for their sections. The only other such asterisk in the poem falls at the end of part I, after the bitter vaunt of Arnaut Daniel, Dante's contemporary: *I am Arnaut who gathers the wind. . . .* Matthias reproves him: "Who was Arnaut to gather the wind?" The hikers there are Eliot and Pound with rucksacks, on the roads that brought them to Excidieul, where a fragment of the old castle wall, lodged in the new one, still shows a bas relief: *the wave pattern cut in the stone.* Finis Part One; the poem therefore has two waves, this one in masonry and the other pushing out from a blast. Each closes a major part of the text.

All of this is bona fide design and construction, and bravo. What I hesitate to add is that the three asterisks appear to do business with it from one angle, the *compos-stella* angle. Asterisks, we easily forget, are stars. Given Matthias's long-honed skill with refrains, and now the nested progressions (out to *the end after the end* here for the first time) which result from his listening closely to his poem, then it is either by chance or by design that the first asterisk ushers in *two* poets, Pound with Eliot in 1920, walking the roads of Provence near Périgord, who anticipate the later entrances, under *two more* asterisks, of the spectral poet of El Cid with a horde of ghost pilgrims, and finally John and Diana Matthias, *both poets* crossing the Puente la Reina. The carved wave arrives with the first star; the blast wave spreads over the last two. Prudently, I hesitate to push the matter. Yet should I also not welcome a touch of high wit in this gesture? Candidates for the polestar have come and gone with the ages. They too are pilgrims. Should we exclude them from the pattern here? Who is JM to pull down the stars? He may, however, assiduously be following them.

I leave the discernment to my reader. Construction as wit would be no mere grace note in a poem about walking the star routes and listening, in a big way, to one's own poem because it means what it's saying, here about regrounding and there about an ear for the ur-silences. The anonymous singer behind the poem of the Cid parallels Matthias, who arranges for both himself and the old jongleur to cross the same bridge, near the end and then at the end, reaching the end of the earth (Finisterre). But Matthias also arranges for a stationary wave in stone and the enormous blast wave from abandoned ammo to end the first and last parts of his Carmen. One soundless wave stays put, while the big-bang sort of wave, destructive-creative in this poem, fades but never quite stops, also resonating with certain gnostic creation myths, notably that of Valentinus (nearly elected pope but then thrown out) in which the primal pair at origin point are *Abyss* and *Sige*, depth and silence.

Hoc / Go listen; and go figure. Davenport's assessment—*objective and clear*—may still, from the writer of "Ernst Mach Max Ernst," host the reverberant, rock-'n'-roll fade, quantum-wave, sorrow-and-release aspects of a unified reverberant field. "A page is essentially a texture of images" (374). Ernst's style grew from discovering that "quotation can be eloquent beyond its original statement, and can release meanings concealed in the original" (377).

Kith are known as neighbors are known. Familiar and trustworthy, like old cloth that rumples rather than folds. When Davenport commended the "Compostela Diptych" as being "objective and clear," he added: "He has refined the narrative and speculative poem." Neither one nor the other, but both, though not necessarily *kith*. Davenport preferred to make compositions as *collections of images*: in re the "Compostela Diptych," that would mean seeing the section layout as more collage than sequence—even with pilgrimage and military slogging in view. GD would not insist on violating the narrative and speculative elements with this preference, but neither would he look past the formal and processual kinship of the three bits we have just worked with. Not *struck* and seeing stars, but seeing the stars within that punctuation, with their latent navigational fix in the images. Which mark first the fear of death (rucksacked Eliot trying to shock rucksacked Pound) and then nearly meeting death (Soult and Ney's armies rumble in, then are followed by lines from *El Cid*, section 128, the torture episode, with the Cid rebuking Avengalvon the Moor, who has taken the Cid's two daughters hostage and prepares to scourge them in the desert). The blow dealt to Matthias by his daughter's defection, and implicitly the guilt at having somehow precipitated it, we know from the epilogue; the application, not from motives shown in *El Cid* but from their lacerating effect, pokes through the old lay here. "Hoc Carmen Audite" follows hard upon, and what we hear (after our second reading) is, "Navigate by the wound, steer by *its* star." Asterisk as star as wireless: we are reading clusters of motifs whose images release navigational signals as audio cues.

Matthias's actual evolution since then has occurred first in the ear, not the eye, on the scale of the single word in *An Automystifistical Plaice* and the ricocheting phrases and nonce terms, ironic and not, in *Revolutions: A*

Collaboration. ("Horseshoe or dingbat, Sir oh just the one / he thought, even if a hoarsepshaw. . . . / Master Craft, I swear // . . . pitching high and inside . . . // However, / *He Who Finds a Horseshoe* fires a synapse begs a question / but in time bags his quarry. . . ." (54). The neurological cue is a ringer in two senses: poetics now may ping steadily on core human ground, aiming continually at the spiking membrane of the synapse. Sound locked in silence, perhaps?—at any rate, the nerve net seethes within and also beyond hearing ("My brain is a thousand bees."— Yvor Winters) as chemical transfers vital to us pour through the scene. Eric Kandel their Virgil will guide you with diagram and summary (passim: serotonin and protein synthesis ride these tiny blast waves). Therefore, while the eye's diagrams remain essential, it is instead our radar, working in Matthias's *silence before silence*, that trawls for the foxfire of neuronal hum. Therefore too, *hoc dendron audite*: these meager pointers of mine derived from Matthias's progression over the past two and one-half decades stalk the image as morpheme; the image cedes primacy to an aural realm because only there does one "hear the roots speaking together" (Pound, Canto XLVII) while also kindling our functioning.

    The fulcrum image in the "Compostela" coda, of the encompassing and fading blast wave, hugely heralds the mini-downbeat in our, this innermost of theatres. In fact, it takes several bridges to get there, as the poem indicates, and a brace of struggling poets to cross them, under changing polestars. Is it because Matthias got that down, with no small degree of intermixed suffering, that his later work takes up the ripple-fire winking through our neural network along with tiny blast waves from the neuronal cell? The several bridges and the six centuries of poetics crossing them? Well, not bad, not bad at all: *that kind of work is the bridge, the one crossed repeatedly.*

The refrain, like an early wireless, anticipates these later evolutionary progressions. Repetition evolves into extensions from this venerable ground, species-old, not as item-by-item words or phrases but as element-by-element nodes *within* the word or phrase. The hemistiches in the old lays were not of equal length or rhythmic pattern; line 2 of the Latin version of *El Cid*, the *Carmen Campidotoris*, reads: *Paris et Pyrri, nec non et Eneae.* The pleasure found in that variation, standard in the poem, we readily note en route, as we track a guitarist's glissandi into or out of certain pitches. Which quietly tickles us, signaling that the performer molds and stretches the framing we coinhabit, which repeats wave, not quantum, fluidly sheltering a migratory letch to squeeze into the heart of it all, through the motor's very windings.

In what Matthias calls "perhaps the most extravagant poem I've ever written," namely "An Automystifistical Plaice" (*Five American Poets* 85), one of the short lines abruptly transmits one such quivering glide: "the plaice is in your face." (The pre-title already had done so—"Working Progress, Working Title [Automystifistical Plaice]"—by squeezing together self-mystification, a tease on work, and the mystical and statistical with something distinctly fishy.) Back to that title in a moment; but first, the statistical dissolution of clearly demarcated pitches or intervals was intended in the notorious premiere of *Ballet Mécanique* used in the poem (George Antheil's sixteen synchronized pianos, alongside three on-stage glissando-keening airplane engines with wooden propellers). The plaice would be, per JM's abrupt cue, situated across a comparable array of wavelengths in the audience (seated and/or reading): (1) You are *eating* the fish. (2) The poetic games of course are sometimes bilingual *plays/plaice* on words. (3) The place/plaice itself, even that—the locus amoenus—is *in your smile*, your amusement at such puns themselves, or at the fluid versus the hammered (engine versus piano), all as *neuronal crossfires* kindled by punning. And (4), at least one of several ultimate ancestors for vertebrate evolution is a fish: therefore, the two-billion-year-old human being is *carrying the fish into our living faces*.

The carnivalesque is *one* thing, we assume—and at issue here is precisely our habit of keeping it distinct, entered with relief and exited when the signal subsides. JM all but says to us across the span of his writing, "In learning how to listen to my own poems, I have been led to experiment with pushing you, my auditors, to stay with me across the arc of the glide, the slide through pitch values: *hoc carmen audite!* for both me and you, but with a smooth, almost transition-free continuity which at certain points brings you up short. Which is natural at first: but you'll get past that."

"Automystifistical Plaice" takes us to summer camp for a workout with JM's version of those sound-creaming airplane engines. In what sense does that development follow in train, by X years, "Compostela Diptych"? It is a *sound* question, in both senses of that word. In the coda to section VI's idiolectal doxology, we are ushered into the velvet seating of a soundproof cosmic amphitheater

> in the stillness

> before anything was still, when nothing
> made a single sound and singularity was only nothing's
> song unsinging . . . aphonia

> before a whisper or a breath, aphasia
> before injury,
> aphelion of outcry without sun . . .

which in hindsight—or no, in after-hearing—pushes us toward the background, or the ground that can be sensed for a brief interval after hearing the jongleur's melodiously barked AOI! Sensed, because that cue ruptures the flow, marking the break-in of bare attention for a brief interval.

Let me put it this way, now that we are summing up: the ground of poetics can be tagged as *no single way* of proceeding, or attending, or hosting performance; but it can, and maybe ought to, be *that circularity of conditions which fosters them all.*

One analogue for that basis would be the latent state of the nerve cell both before and after the 70-millivolt signal which renders its membrane permeable. What goes around comes around in such ground. And while neurology can always be boxed and wrapped by our mental operations—the piggy-backer's delusional privilege—that circulation itself, like Pindar's danced circle for his victory songs, already allows for movement on every scale, as in Pythian 8: "I will be small among the small, / great among the great. The spirit embracing me / from moment to moment I will cultivate, / as I can and as I ought" (173). The easing climax of JM's coda is thrilling in part because it includes us in that elastically self-regulating and grounding circle:

>after the end of the end,

>I, John, walked with my wife Diana
>down from the Somport Pass following the silence
>that invited and received my song

>after Europe's latest referendum. ("A
>Compostela Diptych" pt. II, sec. VI)

That amusingly deflationary tailpiece serves to bracket—fittingly—the briefly majestic-slash-human note followed by the odic note of homage to source or poetic ground, which both invites and receives our cantilenas. One ping of that, or one clearing blast and a closing ping, are already too much in our seculum of voting bigged or rigged: hear that then pass on, viator; the circle opens and closes at the behest—as call and as welcome, both—of cosmic and inner silences.

Listen to this poem! JM shows us how to listen, not by celebrating the victories of Hieron of Syracuse, but by dropping into the signal zone *as such:* before either threshold excitation or repose, paradoxical with respect to sequencings in time, to the place or wavelength of both donation and reception, to birth and death. What emerges from this place is blown free eventually—*strewn* indeed—as poems, to be sure; though what follows very soon are plebiscites, the politics that takes and gives ground with banner and megaphone. Matthias's touch of wit about this all-too-human frequency-stepdown in sequencing—the way things go—acknowledges the proximity of poetic ground to the contested ground of factions and powers. Witnesses from Plato to Hobbes, Voegelin, Arendt, and Patoçka watch him tip that wink in their direction; they know that his gesture does not come at the expense of a corresponding ground for the polis.

The poem's way with regrounding goes for speech as basis, as much or more than for political life. That preference has huge implications for politics, but also for thinking and speaking (wait, Sokrates!). Matthias does not choose—instead he compels the matter to hang open to deeper opening. Once again to the enormous blast, then, from detonated munitions magazines near Coruña and Santiago. The previous section ends with Franco's rise; therefore the auditory illusion is a nice or exacting one, making an episode from the Carlist Wars, with Napoleon entering from the wings, seem to shatter the uneasy quiet of the 1930s. Yet the imaginative power of this stroke is such that it sends a cymbal crash out over the whole poem, which tallies goods and evils from chorused sources, and winds from the dead, so as to mound up, disentangle, clarify, examine lovingly, see through, hear again, and listen to for the first time, the ground of poetic speech in the West. As in: "a strange boat arrived off

Finisterre . . . // (Or so they say. Or so they said / who made the book)" (pt. I, sec. II). Or as in,

> So it began. So they said it had begun.
> A phase (a phrase (a moment in
> the spin of some ephemeride (a change
>
> not even in the modes of music
> from the Greek
> to the Gregorian . . . (pt. I, sec. II)

Those nesting unclosed parentheses open onto the deep background to shifts in intonation, performance, or the accretions of sacred legends. The handbook tables of planetary motions will slip up on us before they will tell us why. Strains old and older, qualification on qualification? Well, of course, but: *Play it, Sam. Play it.* (Bogey did not say *Play it again,* but he did repeat his *request* to the mournful Peter Lorre.) The repeated gesture here—a modern historian's scrupulous notations on oral tradition—resists wedding itself to contemporary hermeneutic skepticism.

Our evidence for the that shortfall is the final section's structure, which pours comprehensive sound, including oral legends across the generations, into inclusive and peaceful silence, in the subtly constructive spirit that one can trace right through Matthias's various strands of subversion. Beginnings? No end of them. But which is the one at hand? The munitions blast in the poem's final section, through cascading stanzas, rocks the bells in Santiago's churches, on ships at sea, in houses and in the heads Basque shepherds. "Then in the high

& highest places everything was still. // As it was in the beginning" (pt. II, sec. VI).

As readers will see when they dig in: Matthias ushers them across the sill from the penultimate to the final section as surely as a theater usher with his flashlight:

> *Viva la Muerte*'s the Falangist song.
> Lorca's murdered; Machado & Vallejo promptly die.
>
> Trusting neither Mithra nor St. James, his eye
> on anarchists in Barcelona,
> Franco summons mercenary Moors to save the church.
>
> VI
>
> In the high places, they could hear the blast.
> Ships rocked on the sea,
> the houses at Coruña shook on their foundations
>
> when the ammunition stores were blown.
> At Santiago, bells that had burned Almanzor's oils
> rang from the shock of it . . . (pt. II, sec. V–VI)

The likelihood is that momentarily we overlook Franco's intention to crush Barcelona, even associating him with the Muslim conqueror's sacrilege with those bells, and likewise associate the ammo dump with some defeat of the Popular Front—why not?—near the coastal city north of Santiago, Coruña. But a peek into the history reveals that the large munitions pile left by General John Moore's fleeing British army, hounded by Napoleon's General

Soult, whose artillery killed Moore shortly before the successful escape to the ships, was detonated about ten miles south of Coruña and therefore about twenty miles north of Santiago. Matthias's swiftly marshaled cues, like one of Bonaparte's cavalry moves, lure us one way while the main force goes in the other. Chances are good that we go for the feint, missing the likelier ("correct") reading only after checking in with our scouts.

The feint here by Matthias is apt to his larger aims: the point is less to peg a particular munitions blast—there have been others too—and more to open awareness toward a prolonged dilation, one that takes the attentive ear on a long Rock-'n'-Roll fade, across more than three pages, into the utmost reaches of stillness. To bind a spell, first one must master the trick of creating it, which artful repetitions through the entire section manage by *sounding out the disappearance of sound*. Unsaying by agensaying—and setting aft before fore, indeed reverse-prioritizing decreation over creation:

> in the stillness
>
> before anything was still, when nothing
> made a single sound and singularity was only nothing's
> song unsinging . . . aphonia
>
> before a whisper or breath, aphasia
> before injury,
> aphelion of outcry without sun . . . (pt. II, sec. VI)

That last triad amply embraces the wounding that impinged while the poem was in process: speechlessness at painful separation, the difficulty of configuring a mysterious distancing, and a Beltane-like conjuring-up of a sun not only farthest from us in its swing but also, inconceivably, gone. Yet countering this decreative triad comes the final product of widest stillness, of voice altogether lost: by happy similitude, the blast and its spreading effects have a cousin in Heidegger's choice of the verb *streuen*—cognate with our own *strew*—for his characterization of metaphysical grounding. What goes around comes around (karma), but what clears ground does so in order to prepare for regrounding, a trope already acceptable to Hesiod's farmers and shepherds.

In real time, as we know, the coda was written around three years after the 1987 itinerary in Spain and France, during or after the departure of JM's troubled daughter. The poem went to press probably late 1990 or 1991. How long the shock of loss and worry persisted we do not know, but the ephemerides for those, like the ones for the births of galaxies, are elastic at best. What Matthias portrays is a genuinely new state, ex nihilo, which equipped him with something like Heidegger's strewn triad for grounding, moving him to frame a doxology: "everything was still. // As it was in the beginning. As it will be in the end"—after which massive scope and after-blast (from within, most of us would add), the Matthiases enter the poem whole: "and after the end of the end // I, John, walked with my wife Diana. . . ." (pt. II, sec. VI).

Robert Archambeau's salute to this turn in the poem is impeccably right. I would add only that the closing catalogue of pilgrimage trails and adjacent routes on foot, on a renewed basis after the sonic clearing, allow JM in retrospect to carry the load he shares as parent and writer *into the decreative field,* which is a post-doctrinal way of saying that the ground had been refashioned autonomously, on out to the rim.

Most of us will recognize this inflection. One loyally carries the load of grief or sorrow, the compunction hypothetical or real (many are the circumstances, but single is the dynamic), until *on its own* the entire burden shifts, reconfiguring itself (one has dined on oneself sufficiently), becoming a different matter to carry thereafter. We do our part, but the alteration also happens over our heads and under our feet. While the facts have not changed, the task and the atmosphere have shifted. Because Matthias does not allude to their missing daughter—the first time was also the last, in the epilogue—he has us stay with the fading blast wave (we are sorting out place and time). The suspension turns into both meaning and structure, as with the crescendo aftermaths in Mahler's slow movements, or after the full orchestra crash that punctuates the last movement of Shostakovitch's Fourth Symphony, initiating a vast diminuendo out to its far rim with fading celesta.

This refrain invokes a primal sound effect about primal soundlessness. And lodged within a miniature refrain—*high and highest*—silently brackets its own comparative, *higher:* altogether, a Russian doll or Chinese box set for the metaphysics of nested ascents, through a clearing as unpredictably timed as its emotional logic was inevitable. Thus, both sounded and silently: as with

Donald Davie's syntax in "Or, Solitude," so here: an enactment of poetry's *metaphysicality*. True, a catalogue is possible for this ending that does not end audibly: the doxological phrase about terminus goes on to embrace—with the silence of the ground of grounds—St. Francis's sermons and songs, the Logos and the Deunde, Ignatian propositions, the Grail legend ("where they say, they *say* / the Grail came to rest"), Mithraic oaths, the bellow of dying bulls, the silence of abbeys, abbots, monks in the fields, sacristy, stores, garden, and copy room, the language of Castilian *juglares,* and then Matthias's own hymn to primordial silence—and finally his homage to their host Delgado-Gomez at Pamplona, and to the ground they walked, ending with the refrain line. Actual ground, with actual song, sermon, and silence, with actual legend, history, theology, and prayer, have been taken up into silence after deafening sound. The deaths of Machado and Vallejo in the preceding section barely precede the noise of that blast; great voicing is dying, and then? Yet however venerable the prototype for the refrains in the final section, their work is to blow the past into a super-dense X with all that damned powder, then open anew from the highest places, loci altissimi, having a total survey of the ground.

And all to one side of the late-Victorian motto of John Ingalls, adopted by air forces worldwide as well as used by Hesse, Harper Lee, Vonnegut, and a Beacon Hill convent in Boston: per aspera ad astra: through hardships to the stars.

JM's coda arrives when voice has been stringently questioned by the third Objectivism, Language poetry.

Aspects of voice had been elevated by W. C. Williams and Olson and O'Hara, but the recent Objectivist ascesis dovetails with the stifling of voice, orality, and other ego vagaries by the deconstructive turn to writing/text. Matthias's particular value is his consistent scrupulosity about texts, both citing and reworking them, while also exploring voicing, notably in poems of some length in the decades following "Compostela." Its coda uses refrain to push one limit—outer reach—so as to reground voicing. Also, functionally, not decoratively, "Compostela" uses refrains as a compact model for reconstellated forms, which in the end are not very many; refrain not as momentary closure but as procedure; refrain anticipating retotalization or renewed return, like the Neo-Platonic epistrophe (homecoming); refrain as the formative impulse in Mandelstam's "Octets," its eyes screwed tight while it floats in space—all of these cohabit in Matthias's post-blast quiet, just when they are needed, in the beginning.

VII
I Canna Hear Ye, Me Darlin†

The coda's path to regrounding needs a broader airing, however, if one is to assess the stakes which it meets and raises.

First, the coda consolidates the poem's firmly quiet and private religious attitude. It inherits little or nothing from Arnold's "Stanzas from the Grand Chartreuse," but does emerge in part from Eleanor Munro's orientation on the up-there/down-here scoping of pilgrimage routes and practices, specifically the fact that pilgrimage typically employs the paced-out route and its astral orientations as the means of a death practice. Her feminine hospitality to the accretions of custom, contradiction, and symbolic density only enhance the showing that the trails work as therapeutic systems, both givers and provers of ground.

"A Compostela Diptych" negotiates a path toward top-to-bottom healing, prospectively collective and synchronistically personal, and the negotiation of that path is itself the structure of feeling which offers good ground. The "Diptych" attaches itself to that structure-as-procedure, the incremental uncovering of consciousness (the historian's "they say") as it works the appointed roads. For precisely in those days when the roads crumble, there one must walk. And precisely those who give testimony about this may be misheard, by either those who take the roads as still given or those who disdain them completely. Neither group grocks this death practice, though they may be superb readers otherwise: witness Paul Fussell's irritated deafness, despite his military experience, to the complex invocation of chivalric materials in David Jones's *In Parenthesis*, a poem in some ways easier to get because its author has declared faith. But then no one ever said that writing en route, *ob via*, would be an obvious matter.

Most of all, the blast wave at first commands attention impersonally yet settles it on Matthias and his wife Diana finally. Plainly, the blast wave clears every ground and then restores them all. It's as necessary as breathing out and then in, or as decisive as exhausting every possible measure only then to discover that each measure has been renewed. All this began to happen for them, not during the actual trek on foot with their Spanish guide Gomez, but later, particularly for JM in the writing. The walk ends not in the direction of Santiago but on the coast, at Finisterre—the end of the earth— fittingly only in retrospect, when the hard turn cast a new slant on their earlier felicity and thereby sustained them in their dismay.

    Secondly, the coda unobtrusively integrates feeling into new forms. One is sheer scope: the whole poem inventories Western European cacophony, slowly enough to touch each part distinctly, but then moves across the bridge of explosion while harmonizing the earlier cacophony and passing into high silence. A subtext progression transits Christian hope while touching the sad contradictions of political Christendom, to bank on hope rather than on any of its formulae. This spacious transit bypasses the individual heart and the mystic's privacy, with feeling for silentium and spes derived from collective experience—the quiet of the communal heart, rarely invoked and in our day scarcely conceivable. The destructive blast prior to this silence sets tragic limits (think of Pindar's "savior and saved alike speared by the lightning flash— / from the gods we must expect / things that suit our mortal minds, / aware of the here and now, aware of our allotment," Pythian 3). Yet a communally legible ground for silence spreads through the poem's closing movement, unto the high places. This structure of feeling steps around Pound's *Cantos*, which reach behind commercial decline and tragedy to the erotic interlude and the Eleusinian mysteries for a silence concordant with justice. "A Compostela Diptych" does not reach behind, but through.

The coda also dilates the whole poem's already slow pace. Gone is the anxiety-ridden flight through the empty space of a language losing its ground, in "Northern Summer." "Diptych" as a whole, through a therapeutic retracing of ground at walking pace, puts the brake on structures of feeling typical of modernist and some contemporary work, whether through the eye's jump-cuts or the ear's subject rhymes. Tony Pinkney writes, "When Deleuze and Guattari declare in *Anti-Oedipus* that 'a schizophrenic out for a walk is a better model than a neurotic lying on the analyst's couch,' they clearly remain within the modernist problematic of Baudelaire's *flâneur* or Woolf's Mrs. Dalloway ambling decentredly through central London" (Pinkney 4). The urban wanderer's courting of collisions, its wavelength of mental speed, descends from Wordsworth and Marinetti or Mayakovsky. At one pole Matthias relishes swift transitions and fold-overs, but not in this pivotal poem. David Jones, dear to JM, notwithstanding his breathtaking moments of scoping, also lingers to polish the spolia and scrape at the deposits. In "A Compostela Diptych" Matthias has moved to recover ground, without Jones's cadenced retards and not losing altitude in the end, and to reduce modernist speed without sacrificing the ability to alter mental space.

A walk that courts caroming impacts is a disguised run, or perhaps a flight disguised as an exploration. What such a near-trot knows, dreads, and yet also excitedly seeks is shock. The aspect of Matthias's coda that tallies with this typical modernist rupture, that is, with the cut and jolting slide of film, poetry, and urban experience (many critics besides Benjamin now elaborate this), is the munitions blast. The whole of "Diptych" moves up to this jolt, then enters an expansive cadence across it. The blast splices two eras, Carlist and Fascist; it both troubles perception with a disconcerting, half-concealed rhyme, and clears away the poem's patient inventory without disaffirming what it clears away. In fact, the aftershock dilates on a loving inventory of Western Europe in its mysterious coherence. The spotting and function of the blast show a modernist structure of feeling deploying classical climax as its doorway into classical closure-in-stillness. What kind of writing emerges from this compound stroke?

Matthias has poised two compositional impulses against each other in a dynamic equilibrium, around a repetition—concretely as two periods of war, artistically as explosive climax and hushed rupture—which then spreads into the coda as a "high and highest" ground. The older poetics of climax and catharsis balances against the modernist rupture of same, across a point whose interior doubling and *trompe l'oreille* (just *when* did that explode?) prevent it from being absorbed by either formal impulse, classical or modernist. The ground traveled by the expanding blast wave is potentially new, although it is old Spain that one hears described; that tension builds quietly behind the description. I know of no other episode in contemporary poetry that manages so much so deftly, with great shock and greater quiet, to ends both sobered and renewed.

The blast inaugurating the coda points to still another grounded transfer: a shift from one sensory mode to the other, from eye to ear. Only Pound anticipates this clearly, with the triangulation among Troubadour song, Greek epic, and acoustic intuition verging on the mystical in his Canto XX. The stakes in this matter are general, grounding movements within sensibility. The shift from eye to ear involves poetics now in a rapprochement with hermeneutics, though in a nonskeptical key, along the lines of prolonged duration and its myths, the "always already" of the theorists and the "sound slender" that Pound hears stretching from Homer's *ligur' aoide* through Arnaut Daniel's *noigandres* or *d'enoi ganres,* to something a contemporary might hear as "too far off to be heard" yet piercingly present. The strong and lovely alternative, Anglo-Saxon in Bunting's "flutes flicker in the draft and flare" (section V of *Briggflatts*), stretches far but does not hang there like a hummingbird. Both Pound and the theorists are after one of the mind's interior waterfalls, always falling.

In his essay on Roy Fisher, apropos "The Cut Pages," Matthias draws on analogies to Fisher's jazz experience, wherein for any member of a band taking the lead the music has already begun. Matthias touches back to Fisher's line in "If I didn't"—where "the poem has always / already started"—and adds a comparison to "Heidegger's notion of language speaking through our listening when, as Gerald Bruns has said, 'nothing gets signified . . . but things make their appearance in the sense of coming into their own'" ("The Poetry of Roy Fisher" 46–47). This mode of appearing is not JM's own, but his phrase about Heidegger's notion of language "speaking through our listening" cues us to retrieve, from the coda to "A Compostela Diptych," our major matter.

Earlier I dealt with Benjamin's Baudelaire, through Rainer Nägele's contention that at the core of modern experience something jarring and decisive happens to the eye. Nägele's accent is not startling, since it caps an emphasis that begins at least with Blake. What Matthias notices in Fisher's "The Cut Pages," which comes out of Fisher's visual sensibility, he notices by way of the ear, not the eye. Between jazz analogies to ongoing, already-begun material, and Heidegger's attention to the listening that receives material prior to significations, Matthias moves from the now-classic modern emphasis on seeing in poetics to hearing.

    What do we hear, between the fading blast and the description, in the coda to the "Diptych"? We listen for more than we hear; we may find ourselves catching strains of a new grounding for speech, "too far off to be heard" but on its way; that is, in the terms of Matthias's own phrase about Heidegger, our listening goes past the language that is present to become a quiet speaking of its own. And when did that begin, such listening? The double figure of the blast, its *trompe l'oreille,* is there to keep our answer nimble. The theoretical phrase "always already," from Fisher, stems from Continental hermeneutics; Nathaniel Tarn nicely parallels this usage with the more intuitive practice of Eluard (*poésie ininterrompue*) and the necessary illusion of ongoing thrust (Tarn 339, 346). Such asides on the phrase are to the main point, however, for the classic shock experience of modernity, which renders the eye a template for a jarred, stilled, narrowed consciousness alert but reactive, enjoys full compensation when one can move to the ear's steadier, potentially seamless and continuous poetic. And that is what Matthias has done, first in a tentative, dialectical fashion in "Northern Summer," where the void of the moving eye vies with suspensions of the halfdreaming ear to frame a possible regrounding, and then decisively in the coda to "Diptych," where a climactic hearing opens the poem's closure out into the territory of its regrounding. A generative listening, parallel to a generative silence, has always already been at work; only thus may a regrounded speaking emerge from it.

Anyone at all familiar with modern philosophy will know that the stakes in the always-already game have mounted high indeed. Early in the joust Paul Ricoeur tried to wedge open the intrinsically closed hermeneutical circle where it "proceeds from a prior understanding of the very thing that it tries to understand by interpreting it," contending that this closure also blesses one with an opening.

> I can still communicate with the sacred by making explicit the prior understanding that gives life to the interpretation. Thus hermeneutics, an acquisition of "modernity," is one of the modes by which that "modernity" transcends itself, insofar as it is forgetfulness of the sacred. I believe that being can still speak to me—no longer, of course, under the precritical form of immediate belief, but as the second immediacy aimed at by hermeneutics. (352)

What this increment of consciousness practices forgetting is of course another circle, that enclosure or zoning-off (thus *locus sacer*) for the purposes not of interpretation but encounter and special handling. Poetry converges with hermeneutics in Ricoeur's spirit whenever it lets its hunger for primary immediacy and *locus* be consistently haunted by unavoidable second immediacies—when, in Yeats's phrase, it remembers reality and justice in a single thought. Poetry also starts to do this when it listens for an elusive sound that repeats or sustains itself at the margins of audibility, for such listening moves beyond heard demarcations toward a grounding that no single locus for sound provides. It is Homer's *ligur' aoide*; no, it is Arnaut's *d'enoi ganres*; no, it is distant birdsong; or, it is my wife reading Scott to my children; no, it is my mother reading Scott to me as a child; no, it is the sound of an heraldic bird winging through language. The coda to "A Compostela Diptych" brings this listening to that pitch of mind where memory quickens even while sound fades, where forgetting and remembering get conflated with each other in both a disconcertingly bifocal blast and a pregnant silence, and where what can emerge from listening is the maybe-sound of a possible yet out-of-range ground.

VIII
Hoc Carmen Audite!

The jongleur's higgity-jiggity "Stay awake, now, listen up!" in the Latin *El Cid* I take as an uncanny precursor to the practice, after modernism in English at least, of plucking at one's own guitar on a dump in New Haven. After all, if one doesn't have a half-drowsy living audience, then what could be more useful than words held in the mind? Cheaper than a hand-held phone, and it goes way back. "I hear the roots speaking together" (Pound, Canto XLVII), and the shoots come from nowhere else. The jongleur's command, thus turned on oneself today, means that one's teacher may be lurking in one's own language, and that *poet* does not mean "full author[ity]" but always and at least "the hearer of his or her own word."

Heidegger, like others awestruck by Hölderlin, compared such inward listening to the searching of ground as he had labored to grasp it. Mandelstam, living for years under proscription and the threat of expulsion and death, forbidden *to write*, might easily have heard—had his language been English, in Matthias's hypothesis in *Revolutions*—the ringing in his "horseshoe" daring him to bawl out a "hoarse pshaw" or "raw-edged protest." Thus is the sounding secured by JM the moment that O.M.'s poem "The Horseshoe Finder" has revolved thoroughly *in his own English.* (The translation of Mandelstam's ode by Steven Willett suggests better than some others how often the poem deploys strong, sharp sounds or noise, and Clarence Brown's mapping of the half-subliminal web or "drift" of various sound patterns in the whole group of poems, 1921–1925, demarcates a broad zone of percussive, whooshing, straining, clotting, and related sound clusters.) Willett: "the furious forestless air," "the ragged surface of seas," a forest's "tops . . . clattered beneath fresh cloudbursts". . . "Where shall we start? / Everything cracks and reels. / One word's no better than another, / the earth drones with metaphors. . . . . Thrice blessed, he who guides a name into song, / the song adorned with nomination / lives longer among the others. . . ."

No word is better than any other, I take it, at least in a certain way: in serving as a warehouse of energies, all the way from imitative splashes or rips to the nomen individuum, bearer of patriliny and a shared personal name toward achieved singularity—the very individuation which this "Pindaric fragment" holds high (an illustrious name on its very pennant) it also loses to harsh turbulence. "The air is mixed as solidly as the earth: / One can't get out of it, to enter it is difficult." Presumably, it is also difficult to escort a name into this mix: "Human lips, / for which there's nothing more to say, / Retain the form of their last-spoken word. . . ."

If we needed a reminder at the outset of the twenty-first century, we have it already from O.M. in the early 1920s: saloons are speakeasys but poems are not. The real poems cannot be, for they stay directly answerable to the condition of a disturbed and transposed spirit, a real roarer or Brausewind: "One can't get out of it, to enter it is difficult." Therefore, in contrapuntal formation to those conditions, the ability to lodge a victor's name honorably in a poem—such being Pindar's vocation in his portion of the few hundred years of danced choral lyric—though it may call on movement and music, it will be sustained chiefly toward one end, the lodging of a name in the light of long-shared mind. That is the venerable, renewable warrant—but actually possible nowhere in fact for O.M., so far as he could see.

Matthias gets precisely to that nowhere in his final poem in "On Five Words Englished from the Russian," from "Horseshoe Finder," as drawn on in *Revolutions*. Like the great horse reduced to its bones, his trio's dealings with Mandelstam likewise probe at constituent elements. Neither an autopsy nor a rag-and-bone shop affair, this inventory-by-serial reflection, especially within JM's language, gets at darkness askew, or by way of multiple linguistic kedgings. Item by item odd at first, it grows on one. That angularity from Matthias may even come to seem inevitable, in that Mandelstam's parent poem, "The Horseshoe Finder," at mid-stride already pitching toward self-erasure, indeed is the only modern poem, of indisputably Pindaric weight and value, to persuasively rekindle such fire only to snuff itself out. To apply our language for poetic ground here: Matthias listens in on this staggering transmission signal—six ways to Sunday but finally daunted—for promptings toward the lines he will craft while examining himself as he writes several short poems of responsory tribute, including a riff upon Mandelstam's octets in "The Age."

    I know just enough about this territory to realize that going any further toward the Russian dimension, or even JM's dealings with it, would be folly. What I can say in closing is that this most recent enterprise by Matthias, even in close collaboration with his mates, develops further his repeated forays into sounding the ground within poems, the "Listen up!" basis of poetics, active as a method once the lays sung at courts in the European late Middle Ages could be audited later with a dialectical ear.

    Mandelstam's ode and JM's five responses instance a combined audition of poetic ground—particularly since in his ode O.M. too puts his ear to the ground of his own language, deriving his final wasted stance in that decisive ode precisely from what he hears there. JM does likewise, but in a different world and to quite other ends. Their appointed partnership, however, is an angular, strangely affecting stethoscopic survey of a spookily shared collective basis, ours as much as that of our grandfathers.

Matthias's practice on this basis in *Revolutions*, rather than arbitrary, is the classic method of divination turned inward on his poetic means. The haruspices in this instance constitute a séance, both O.M. and JM in league, only JM aware that he is consulting the shades or the chances not solo but as a partner. Legend has it that the YiJing, which JM briefly invokes, was invented on the floors of a comfortable prison by the great royals of their age. In the partnership which I fantasize for O.M. and JM, that practice is devoutly pledged to the particulars of destiny and circumstance, including their actual biographical records, one a spirit master and the other a living seeker. The arbitrary but fated arrays of both personal life and the historical situations for both would be live questions still to JM. Diviners are devout listeners, placing their ears directly on the breast of occasion, working only with what returns to them as the voice of the case that is.

Item: if a *hoarse pshaw* crosses over from *horseshoe* at the language interface found by JM in Mandelstam's title, "The Horseshoe Finder," then in those focused shallows where he is kedging for workable depth, so be it: that finding is inherent, or navigable, lending voice to the fated array at that time and location (in this case JM's poem). The finding thus transposed over the divination frame—the parent poem's language, translated into one's own—stipulates at that juncture several readings: in this case, one's devout commitment to the chances among several kinds of interface, translated or carried-over as-is, allow JM to hear the rasping dismissal (hoarse pshaw) of his boyhood tyrannical camp counselor. Or the rasping decree against Mandelstam's fate by Stalin's flunkies, and Stalin himself. So be it, to both possibilities—in spite of the yawning discrepancy between JM's instance and Mandelstam's. That gap invites study, of course, not credulity—and so begins the investigative task, of a kind ridiculous to settled folk who ridicule the whole business and walk away, but skin-crawlingly, tummy-turningly engaging to JM and his kind, who sniff meaning somewhere ahead. It is not for some silly old reason that poetics is called *finding*.

No other way remains available for speaking to one's own occasion. The grammar of occasion takes the foreign language into one's own, and then kedges it through the aperture of divination, measured by ear: nothing could be starker, and few things more demanding. The crabbed and ungainly facts, unforeseeably penetrating routine assumption and habit, serve the exactingly just-so. Parts of "The Age" by a Russian Jew under surveillance in the 1930s, rendered in one's own cramped phrases, move in ungainly ways precisely because *the unheard-of* emerges necessarily from the poetics of one's ground *made thus audible*, especially in a vis-à-vis with the translated or transposed lineaments of one's own childhood camp experience: disproportionate, even bizarrely miniature, yet just that dimension discloses what must be spoken for and confronted in this vis-à-vis. Therein, the ore to be mined, therein the ungainly treasure.

To repeat, nothing is more objective than divinatory procedures—to reinvoke Guy Davenport's estimate of the Compostela poem, "objective and clear." The agility required for moving between literary and divinatory domains is not Olympic, however, because both result from consultations with a range of powers within reach and handling but not within our power arbitrarily to command. Within that spacious conjunction rest both our humility and our creative scope. The final octave in JM's "Epilogue: The Age," in responsory to Mandelstam's poem, begins,

> *Assailed* is a word. And so is *asylum*.
> Thrice blessed is he who puts a name in his poem:
> *Osip. Anna. John.* Twenty sticks drop down from
> Giants playing six dimensional YiJing.
> But also blessed is he who writes *refrain, refrain.*
> Sing me, sergeant, to the unscheduled train.
> (*Revolutions* 108)

Security on this reading (in the first line) rests squarely on our vulnerability. One appropriately vulnerable thing for a poet to do, therefore, is to lodge his own name in the poem in which he translates the work of the poet who recommends exactly that dare. But Mandelstam's and Akhmatova's and then one's own first name?! The clatter heard next—ominous, high-ironic, as if an acolyte dropping the sacred paraphernalia were Harpo Marx—

comes from a variant on the Chinese divination practices first worked out by the nobles, in prison indefinitely, who employed fifty sticks. The qualifying "But," therefore, forestalls any hubris that might derive from the naming ritual, and from going further with the joke on halting oneself and then submitting to fateful transportation: *Stop, stop!* veteran employer of refrains, Matthias, halt!

    The twenty sticks or yarrow stalks (not the regulation fifty) suggest to me that their clamorous throw-down here inaugurates the last twenty years of Mandelstam's life: officials high in the Soviet state moved in 1928 to undermine him, enforcing tenuous perches in Moscow, Leningrad, and Armenia followed by hard times in Moscow then exile in Voronezh; attempted suicide and two heart attacks preceded the sentence to five years at hard labor in August 1938. He was dead by December (Brown, chapter 8, 121–34). If I am correct in my surmise, then Matthias showers his own situation with the din of that suffering, rattling the little auditorium of his own camp memories (an *asylum* by contrast) with what had *assailed* Mandelstam. More: the Giants assail JM's asylum with twenty sticks about presumptuous self-naming, and yet surely enough, with grim comic touch the root carried from Greek into Latin, *Gigas*, names a person, so that another name enters the poem, mugged up from myth and fate rather than by Matthias's own hand.

    The sober joke in all of this, jelling in the stem within *sergeant* and the Middle English *geant*, and melding with others from Latin, Greek, and French, is the legal variant on several stems from Latin and the Romance languages: *servientem* or public servant, by way

of Latin *servus* or slave, onward to serf and sergeant—
from the Indo-European root *swer*, "perhaps to guard"
(Partridge). All of which lets one see that the passage to
security through extreme vulnerability continues; it must
go on proceeding that way in order to go on at all. The
gnomic discovery of asylum within the condition of being
assaulted issues into the comedy of venturing to name
oneself in a heroic elegy. The sticks specifically allude to
O.M.'s fate while aiming directly at JM's dare at naming
himself in respect to that fate. The inquirer therefore turns
to self-corrective refraining, for the moment consigning
poetic authority to that public servant of servants, Sarge
of the transit camps, the last poet to offer his voice
("Sing me," JM implores) in the entire suite of poems in
Revolutions.

Mandelstam's "Horseshoe Finder" commences
a second time internally, with a racket in strophe three
("Where to begin? / Everything cracks and shakes"),
growing quiet again only by strophe eight (the ode
closes with strophe nine). Given the high stakes placed
on praise-naming not only in Pindar but also in any
poetics of regrounding now pledged to *listening to itself*,
Mandelstam's ode offers the benchmark instance of
installing a name. How Mandelstam listens in on his own
progression therefore is material to its purpose. Strophes
three through eight write the full score of hearing the
ground spell out its cadence: initial achievement and
heroic naming, but terminal retreat twenty-seven lines
later (uncovering the horseshoe as relic, the iron omega
of anonymity). Therefore to lodge a name in an ode,
explicitly a Pindaric fragment and Mandelstam's only

poem in irregular meter and line lengths, becomes its acme function. And in this poem that name is *Neaera* (a dozen Neairas populate Greek legend; Brown-Merwin's note alerts us to its classical nickname usage as "sweetheart"). The most likely Neaera or "newly risen" would be the Thracian Okeanid and springs-nymph for the river Stryon, her husband. (Sru, the IE root, is stream or flow; in Thracian, struma is river, and in Turkish becomes "the black waters.") Mandelstam's tactic proves to be, literally, a washout; it *goes without saying*, then, that such saying unintentionally becomes self-emptying: inaudible, the iron omega hangs as doorframe decor, for luck (German Lücke, "exit") over a passage point—and also as the token of an emptied mouth. Remarkably for our inquest here, this strophe inventories a slow holocaust of any regrounding for poetics, a cascade of depletion through four of the five senses into inanity (smell, touch, hearing, and meaning through both hearing and seeing), which converts the medium of air into earth, and replaces the sound of a name with metallic ambivalence, intense inanity resounding through murky obscurities. The fifth strophe prepares the way for the only name installed in this ode (Clarence Brown and W. S. Merwin's version follows, with the strophe numbers added in brackets):

> Thrice blest is he who puts a name in his song. [4]
> The song graced with a name
> outlives the others.
> She may be known among her companions by her headband
> that preserves her from fainting, from too-strong numbing odors

whether of the nearness of the man,
the fur of a powerful animal, or simply
the smell of savory rubbed between hands.

Sometimes the air is dark as water, and everything in it [5]
is swimming like a fish,
fanning its way through the sphere,
through the dense, yielding, scarcely warm
crystal with wheels moving in it, and horses shying,
and Neaera's damp, black earth, that is turned up afresh
every night by forks, tridents, mattocks, plows.
The air is as deeply mingled as the earth;
you can't get out of it, and it's hard to get in.

A rustling runs through the trees as through a lush
    meadow. [6]
Children play jacks with bits of animals' backbones.
The frail tally of our age is almost done.
For what there was, thank you.
For my part, I made mistakes, got lost,
came out wrong. The age clanged like a golden ball,
hollow, seamless, held by no one.
When it was touched it answered 'yes' and 'no'
as a child answers
'I'll give you the apple,' or 'I won't give you the apple,'
with a face that matches the voice saying the words.

The sound is still ringing, though what has caused it
is gone. [7]
    The stallion is lying in a lather, in the dust, snorting,
    but the tight arch of his neck recalls

the stretched legs racing,
not just the four of them
but as many as the stones on the road
coming alive by fours
at each bound of the fiery pacer.

Therefore   [8]
the one who finds a horseshoe
blows the dust from it,
rubs it with wool till it shines,
and then
hangs it over the door
to rest,
not too be made to strike sparks from the flint again.
Human lips
    that have no more to say
keep the shape of the last word they said,
and the hand goes on feeling the full weight
even after the jug
has splashed itself half empty
    on the way home.

What I'm saying now isn't said by me. [9]
It's dug out of the ground like petrified wheat. . . .

    Already in the fourth strophe, the poem that honors a name figures as a Greek maiden with a headband (which came into use in Greece during Pindar's lifetime), which here is apotropaic: it protects her—that is, shields the poem that celebrates a name—from yielding to lust, animal heats, or hunger (that is, it preserves both poetic tact and aim). Normally this spellbinding function would shield from ruin all those poems, like Pindar's, that celebrate individual prowess or achievement. But this "Pindaric *fragment*" testifies to a shattering force, a political and social inversion which violate the wellsprings. Air turns subaqueous, in which the intact earth at the spring of Neaera is heaved into this tossed salad of opposites that annuls orientation. Mandelstam had already written in 1922, in "On the Nature of the Word," that culture was at root philological, and that Russian rather than being Slavic, "is a Hellenistic language" (*Complete Critical Prose and Letters* 120). Naeara polluted, then, marks the wastage of both Russian speech and cultural coherence. With her compromise in this poem, the poetics of honorable naming, as the carrier of such treasure, is pitched into a nearly inaccessible, imprisoning medium. Thus reads Mandelstam's scan of the early Soviet rollout: the terminal echoes and empty vessels cannot begin to speak, and compressive turbulence—that is, a captured and betrayed revolution attacking culture at its linguistic root—leaves one with mere outlines of voicing before the fact of the unspeakable.

    Most to the point is the philology of self-audition. Mandelstam not only dramatizes the failure of apotropaic measures taken in earnest (honorable naming) which end in his own spent value, like battered antique coinage. He also riffs on a cascade of sound patterns, from the fourth through the ninth strophes, which resonate with this drastic fate. Clarence Brown's studies of the image threads and sound clusters as "drifts" in Mandelstam's verse make this factor perceptible. One needs to keep in mind the rope-dancer's kind of balance demanded at this level of the art: yes, the writer chooses much of what comes into play, but much—perhaps more—is in play from the large, much older, still living partner, the tensile, lively rope—the multi-stranded, internally communicating language.

Brown's pages on this poem let one select among the sound clusters running through it, the strongest perhaps being *khr* (which is part of a larger cluster including *shr:* thus zapa*kh* she*r*sti [furry hide] in l. 43, or ve*rkhush*kami [forgetful] in l. 23). In strophes seven, eight, and nine the following playout of two elements in the drift, at risk and at stretch, stitches many things together: in strophe six, line three (cumulative l. 55) comes *khr*upkoe (fragile): "The frail tally of our age is almost done," followed by strophe seven's dying stallion in l. 65 by *khr*apit (in the dust). In l. 67, so*khr*aniaet (recalls [the racing outstretched legs]), and then by l. 81 near the end of strophe eight, so*khr*aniaiut (keeps the shape [of the last word] they [the lips] spoke). Lines 67 and 81, employing the same verb, echo a preservative action—a rear-guard measure, stretched across two strophes—mounted against overwhelming force. The reiterated verb brackets the dying stallion in six with the motionless lips in seven, an audible stitch for two images of curved agony and futility (the translation is Brown's own in his study):

> The stallion lies in the dust, in a lather, and snorts,
> but the sharp curve of his neck
> recalls his racing with legs outstretched. . . .

*

> Human lips,
>   that have nothing more to say,
> keep the shape of the last word uttered. . . .

This kind of image-and-echo collaboration illustrates what Brown often finds in what he calls Mandelstam's drifts. In our terms it results from the poet's consistently giving ear to what the language cannot avoid uttering, whether in texture or sense, if it is to lead the way home.

This poem more than any other modern masterwork may set the degree-zero mark for a philology of listening-*in* for guidance toward the next step. *Hoc carmen audite!* turns into a fourth-dimensional pretzel or Klein bottle, returning one's voice as something like, *Shut up shop? The shop itself has shipped out.*

Or perhaps, *Cut your losses, rub out your name, leave town.* For surely, if one has been made less than oneself, then one's name too has come into question, perhaps even has gone. Intervening between these two markers for Mandelstam—hospitality to the honored name and a name's near-obliteration—are the brassy clangs of one's appointed era (a vast sphere "held by no one") with its infantile sing-song ambivalence, and the ample but empty vessels of communication. In their wake waits a doorway over which hangs a horseshoe's iron omega (once clanging, now silent), a mouth retaining the shape of its last utterance, and the ghostly weight of the jug left in one's hand: a relic totality, a mouth gone south, and spectral inertia, all cups for a gone quid.

Therefore, in reprise but this time with feeling: the ninth strophe enunciates the delayed Q.E.D., that what I seem to be saying is ventriloquized by seeds turned stony in the earth, which has been churned up and strewn into the wellsprings. Not that O.M. stopped writing. Yet this exceptional poem he printed three times, in the trio of books that appeared in the mid-to-late 1920s. The fact that he could no longer quite hear himself at a certain pitch—one's own name as mysterium would be one way of putting it—meant that his chief part in living lay hamstrung, and with it the culture's capacity to listen. The philology or poetics of hearing one's own poems is neither child's play, that game of knucklebones with a horse's vertebrae, nor a career exercise. It is the thing itself. In that respect Matthias's bilingual pun on Mandelstam's title—a hoarse pshaw from horse shoe, a harsh dismissal sounding from within the emblem of finality and good fortune—is apt because of the confrontations upon which it insists. Or due to the findings and their finders: **Nashedij podkovo**, horseshoe finder. First there was the original face-off between Mandelstam and the furious dictator, the defender of philology *as* God-saturated awareness opposed to the former seminarian turned atheist dictator who finally shrieks, *Kill him!* And now there is JM confronted by a rasping demurrer within his own language against his rendering anything at all from O.M.'s Russian: *It's not that you'll murder it, you'll simply make a cacophony of Mandelstam's fatalistic fadeout.*

Both derivations deliver thoroughly nasty occasions, and yet just therein lies the opportunity, just there the imperative for engagement, however ungainly and "complex" in the manner of "Plaice." Divination by ear is all of JM's philology in this case. Maximal focus and pressure are placed upon minimal means, to produce orientation and guiding relationship while retaining traces of the road taken (kedged progressions on the charts, and precise intonations from the auditing of one's own language, particularly as it modulates O.M.'s language in translation). Archambeau's ventriloquial adaptation in *Revolutions* of Matthias's way with Mandelstam's lectures on Dante speaks for this central motive: "Essentially an analysis of the nature of poetry, 'After Five Words Englished from the Russian' explains its hybrid character by constantly referring to Mandelstam as the grand strategist of poetic transmutation and hybridization" (68). The clanging fall of those twenty YiGing divination sticks in his final poem on Mandelstam's materials remains Matthias's most condensed praise gesture toward him, a demonstration that he is listening to his own lines while giving close ear to Mandelstam's at the same time. It becomes a duo concertante, with each conductor giving close ear to his ensemble.

Even anecdote points to this auditory dimension of the facts. In her *Music for Silenced Voices: Shostakovitch and His Fifteen Quartets*, Wendy Lesser reports that the composer, bruised from the chilly reception of his Fourth Symphony in late 1936, crept up on the Fifth in 1937 with feline caution. In November came the premiere; Prokofiev wrote to Shostakovich with encouragement, but "the exiled poet Osip Mandelstam—who illegally spent the night in Moscow, risking his soon-to-be-ended life, in order to hear Shostakovitch's latest work—labeled it 'tedious intimidation'" (29). That verdict, rending though it may sound, a hoarse pshaw indeed, testifies to the treasure sought in one's own turns of the ear within one's own medium. If we listen at all to our own language, then we shall also thirst for corroborating efforts in audition, traveling as O.M. did, long and far, to audit-with or overhear a treasured master in this business. Even if it's disappointing!—for even that outcome supplies one measure of the value keenly sought.

Matthias can presume, as a transatlantic American, to set up this probing parallelism in part because Mandelstam was hospitable to America's access to its own language as he was not to Europe's, which since Luther's day has divorced words from their root auras. (Americans, not Europeans, are more likely to find this assessment surprising.) In 1921's "The Nature of the Word" he maintained Dostoyevsky's view that Western European freedom was largely amoral—thus "Europe devoid of philology is not even America; it is a civilized Sahara desert.... America began to act like someone now crazed, now thoughtful. Then, all of a sudden, she initiated her own particular philology from which Whitman emerged, ... behaving like Homer himself, offering a model for a primitive American poetry of nomenclature" (*Complete Critical Prose and Letters* 125, 615). On this view philology, as a literary and moral integral rising from its own ground, can best serve either an offspring culture or a still pre-Enlightenment cousin. On this reading, too, philology abhors European Voltaire and Francophile Ben Franklin but not Whitman.

Such a view helps one to account for the unusual adhesion supplied by Matthias's angular and probing "takes" on the first line of Mandelstam's ode (written in 1923, two years on from this essay), for it is the preservation of access to memory that moves him, his wife's Parkinsonism long since having stirred him to tense the linguistic wire strung between *Aplysia* (Kandel's specimen slug for neuro research) and *Aplasia* (neuronal destruction and occlusion), an organic devolution thus running parallel to the cultural devolution in morale, along with the powers of speech and poetics, marked so vigorously by Mandelstam. What may seem here to be a privately based configuration pertaining to Matthias most certainly extends past that domain to what the Russian Jewish convert denominated, almost interchangeably, as philology and culture.

Archambeau goes beyond JM's opposition of system crash to lively and continuing growth, proposing that with this thrust Matthias "makes a mutation" of the parallel reduction closing in on Mandelstam even as he rendered it: the felled stallion frothing in dust, the millennia-dented coins. Surely Archambeau's advice is effectual: we are to make of Matthias on Mandelstam what Mandelstam made of Dante in his spirited and allusive "Conversation about Dante." That is, one gains access to a quarry for parallel expansions, not reductions, although startling ones: the kids in "Horseshoe" playing knucklebones with the dead stallion's vertebrae in Matthias morph into bullies at the boyhood summer camp he dreaded. Archambeau: "That Dialectic in Matthias? It's something like his DNA" (72), inherited one may add from the same bullying early instruction endured by Robert Graves and George Orwell. These final poems in the collaboration, however, entrust themselves to the other Mandelstam touchstone, displayed throughout "Conversation about Dante"—the transformational effervescence extracted from the exiled Florentine at every turn in that meditation by that person of interest, O.M. This duo—Dante and Mandelstam—can still provoke writers to read their overlapping maps—from the Resurrected and from Bergson—and to note their brands of jet fuel; critical, not skeptical, transmutable and unleaded. Let the games begin.

IX
Round and Round Ground Round Oure Mete and Drink

Since ground in reflective speech is metaphor, and metaphor is the ground of modern poetics, the fetched-in half of the figure invites deft handling.

Like Greek truth, aletheia, German Abgrund contains what it opposes. That is, disclosure encompasses closure or forgetting, and the abyss swallows, or opens into, its ground. Both Greek and German here, in their parallel ways with the humble negative prefix, perform an inclusive and dialectical way of framing reality. A tyro may of course get fascinated with the toy itself and excitedly cry, "Where is the ground? Why, it's in the abyss!" neatly reversing the usual commonplace perception. Thinkers actually imitate this tyro, of course. What I propose in closing is to listen to the overtones of ground in selected usages adopted in the West, so as to carry out Matthias's hint in his coda to "Compostela

Diptych," to see what might come of listening after a loud note has been struck—like the percussion climax in the final movement of Shostakovitch's Fourth Symphony. The note I'll be testing is chora in Greek, locus in Latin, and land, country, and ground in English, all with parallel overtones that point to high sitings with no coordinates on any map.

Psalm 116, verse 9, in the New Jerusalem Bible reads, "I shall pass my life in the presence of Yahweh, / in the land of the living." The Vulgate: *"Placebo Domino / In regione vivorum"* (revised, 1945: *"Ambulabo coram Domino / In regione viventium"*). The range for regione here, from place to land to zone of meaning, parallels that for the Greek chora, which even in Homer is both spot or site and wider region. The range in English for land is similar. What the psalmist counts on is our keeping both limits of that range alive in our hearing; never are we to retreat to primitivizing chora, regione, or land to some piece of gritty dirt alone, thus erasing the tension. Indeed, the English version of the verse's final lobe has passed into common higher usage; it favors feeling for life, not real estate. Now the life of chora in Christian thinking has gone more or less into the back cupboard in an old kitchen, so that what we risk overlooking is the key linking step in the idea's development toward a nonlocatable grounding. A notable example is the pair of inscriptions in the Church of the Chora's mosaics of Christ and the Virgin Mother, from fourteenth-century Constantinople. The inscription near Christ alludes to our verse from Psalm 116: IS XS HE CHORA TO ZOONTON [Jesus Christ the land of the living]. The parallel inscription for his mother reads, METER THEOU HE CHORA ACHORETOU [The Mother of God, (dwelling-) place of the placeless (uncontainable)]. A window opens in Mary's heart-space to show the infant Christ; this image typifies the Orthodox icon which symbolizes patient human suffering, the instrument of incarnation, and the embodiment of full life: two choras, both paradoxical. Fading symbolization, but persistent life: land or ground in its greater sense is the unifying mystical term, disclosing the abyssal ground that comes into existence in living persons, and paradoxically contains that ground as the open soul, once the God-bearer. With incarnational perception one feels ground within ground, not abyss within ground; or so theology's long passacaglia on Psalm 116 would have it. What incarnational perception would never do is reduce flesh to merest ground, ground as dust alone, for flesh is also *locus sacer,* in tension with the greater chora. While one can track this fruitful tension within the language around chora, ground, and land, now such hearing commonly requires a set of Matthias headphones, post-blast model, type Second Immediacy.

The contemporary philosopher John Sallis weaves impressive reflections around Platonic chorology in "The Politics of the Chora." His focus is also contemporary, turning to forms of the state untrammeled by oligarchy and tyranny. Yet his thinking leaps from the Greeks to Nietzsche, Heidegger, and Arendt, omitting the long Christian chapter, East and West. The tension within chora for Sallis has been smoothed out, incarnation set aside, which empties out being, with not merely spectral consequences.

> Now that the intelligible paradigms have drifted away and become mere stories [Nietzsche's "fable"]—one cannot but wonder whether our time is perhaps preeminently the time of a politics of the *chora*. Assuming that one can still think the outside of being after being has proved a vapor and a fallacy. Now there would be only: images taking place—indeed in a place in which all the markers of certainty would have dissolved. (70)

So much for Ricoeur's ability to hear being. And, welcome aboard, all you flitting simulacra from the pages of Baudrillard! Sallis's chora is skeptical, more in line with Gorgias than with Plato. The missing phase, between Plato and the Nietzschean spread, is the Christian elaboration of ground, person, and polity, a metaphysics that no longer serves. A sound too far to be heard, to stretch Pound's phrase? The end of Matthias's "Diptych" speaks to just such stoppings of the ears. Our positions may not count as much as our sensing does, on a summer evening near the tymbals of the cicada. Such listening might catch what has become inaudible in parts of the ground.

My other context for ground comes from the past 150 years in Western medicine. Earlier I briefly screened the mobile site of the epileptic focus, which can move house. Only temporarily does it lease a piece of our temporal lobes. And so, like the aura which anticipates a seizure, the focus, too, defies a plain answer to the question, "Where is it?"

To go farther, however, the rheumatics specialist Dr. Paul Plotz calls into question the regular medical assumption that a core site, however elusive, can be found for a given disease. That assumption is not only common, but also well-funded: witness the hopes currently pinned on the human genome project. Dr. Plotz points to a disease in his own field which has been tied to flaws in a gene for membrane protein. Several patients with normal genes of this type also display the symptoms of Emery-Dreifuss syndrome; so "where is this disease?" Motor neuron and mitochondrial illnesses challenge location in the same way, as well as several slithery zones "at the solid core" of molecular genetics itself. About diabetes Dr. Plotz asks: is it in the urine, blood, pancreas, islet cell, the end organ insulin receptor, thymus, cytotoxic lymphocyte, the gene for glutamic acid decarboxylase, or HLA molecules? Or several of these? "Or under the slippery rug?" (161).

This sage query has consequences for both the Enlightenment medicine behind current practice and the molecular biology that is changing it. The rational and taxonomic structures animating them both break up on the beachhead of "Where?" For the humanist and poet, that Socratic "Where?" becomes indispensable. Those of us who follow Czesław Miłosz's survey of biology's challenges to humane values across the board will welcome it. "Where?" touches back to Plato's distinction of "there" in chora as grounding from the concrete "there" in the unreflective usages of grounding as land and native ground. The reach within that distinction has consequences not only for biology and medicine—witness

Sallis's smoothing away of the term's tensions in our political context—but also for biology's status as queen among the disciplines. The status retains its perch, while medicine, the family trade behind Aristotle, hermeticizes location. As in ethno-astronomy, the polestar is a traveling man.

Dr. Plotz foresees for medicine a double task: the fragmentation of inadequate, too-inclusive disease descriptions upon findings that refuse to stand in one spot, but also the unification of inquiry around the lived destinies of sufferers. The first task corresponds to the sacrifice of a hypostatized, solid chora to the subtler place of ongoing regrounding. The second task respects subjective testimony, and individual anamnesis and epichrisis, in all their variety, as parts of the grounding for illness—illnesses as lived matters, not only as entities fixable by the nails of causality to the putatively concrete ground of a condition. This once-and-future medical attitude offsets the pressure exerted by biological thinking on the rest of our outlook, for it detaches itself from neither the regrounding of diagnosis nor the narratives that also presume regrounding of some other kind. The grounds can neither be nailed nor ignored with this attitude, for it takes regrounding in stride.

The clarifying reach of that interrogative "Where?" extends into poetics and interpretation as well. At the risk of oversimplifying, I shall trace a few contours thrown into relief by that question, contours that Matthias navigates without concretizing them.

Some of the Language poets, notably Charles Bernstein, lend trust to no language that is not self-contained in its operations, chiefly out of the conviction that a commercial culture sucks dry any rhetoric whatsoever. Therefore, Bernstein's

> insistence that poetry be understood as epistemological
> inquiry; to cede meaning would be to undercut
> the power of poetry to reconnect us
> with modes of meaning given in language
> but precluded by the hegemony of restricted
> epistemological economies....
> [in "formally active" poems] the meaning is not
>   absent or
> deferred but self-embodied as the poem
> in a way that is not transferable to another code
>   or rhetoric (17–18)

The reader may recall Archibald MacLeish's more genteel version of this: "A poem should not mean but be." Bernstein resists "institutionalization of interpretation," yet his affinity with MacLeish marks the institutionalization of one kind of interpretation at mid-century, familiar from the Romantic and nominalist positions of early modern, English Romantic, and Emersonian poetics. The Third Objectivism, in Bernstein's figure, adds to this Gertrude Stein's swing toward the medium itself as guarantor of liberal freedom. In this way the old nominalist redoubt, the inveterate entrenchment in things as guarantor of individual expression in a mass culture, gets taken into language itself. But not all of language: linguistic universals are held in suspicion, because the enemy, too, exploits them. The Third Objectivism, then, converges with skeptical hermeneutics in divesting authorial agency of fuller grounding. Both relocate authority in impersonal reservoirs of potential within linguistic operations, not linguistic universals.

This convergence may seem to insure against the more insidious effects of commercial and political decadence. Yet this same convergence, poetic and interpretive, returns chora to literal ground, the land of language and its operations: a zero-one informational spectral system, not the fluid signaling of neurology. In Provence to this day, the lost homeland is le langage or idiom, but the homeland honored and yearned for in that equation is, precisely, fuller grounding for the straitened spirit of a submerged people, their specifically accented meeting place. By contrast with this, what Bernstein practices is both literal and bloodless. However necessary his attitude, from Blake's Dissenter's perspective to your friend's down the street, something humorless in it construes poetic speech as a reservoir of recombinant differentials that resist convergence and convention (con-venere, meet together) and concession (con-cedere, give over together). Universals are not concessions to someone else's power move in a test of Nietzschean wills. One does not cede meaning (or ground) but enters into various uses of it; nor does one's politics emerge from the facts of the medium itself. Close by the new Objectivists stand the skeptical interpreters, safeguarding indeterminacy for their own reasons, in part to keep language safe from the messy, naive crowd of authors.

Here indeterminacy turns into an abyss factory; the abyss-diver and his back-flips become familiar, even reassuring; the abyss takes on the attributes of ground, an unbudgeable ground of unknowing. It affords negative transcendence to those standing / plunging on / in it; and it harmonizes with an ego psychology capable of indeterminacies but wary of any wider alternatives. Defensive or skeptical self-containment within the medium's horizon courts transcendence negatively because that, in the end, is safer in one's relations with both the Commons and the unknowable. One's "code," however intricate and paradoxical, returns homing to the blessed functions of *the* place, *the* site. A gesture is constantly made toward regrounding, but the chora of any regrounding constantly incorporates dualisms and stabilizes them. The abysses thus opened it has already bred.

From the chora as image theater in Sallis, politically neutral, to the chora as paradoxically literal ground in Third Objectivism and skeptical hermeneutics, it is not a far fetch along the line of exacerbated disillusionment. The ground that has shifted and broken, and with it the corresponding impulse to regrounding that has thrust forward in endeavor after endeavor, are not neighborhood affairs in the parishes of poetry, the other arts, hermeneutics, and political philosophy in the modern university. They stem from the internal collapse of morale, European and Western, in the First and Second World Wars. Regardless of the religious or secular coloring of their identity, these *institutions*, neither exclusively linguistic nor speculative, and arrayed across the board—have gone missing, even within their reconstructed facades. Even those who shrug half-know this; even children sense it. And that fact furnishes every move toward regrounding with its motive energy, whether regressive or brave, whether acknowledged or not.

Such energy sustains "A Compostela Diptych" throughout. The poem clarifies an awareness that we can turn toward various grounding probes underway at least since Paeschendale and the Somme, probes that are seldom aware of each other but that should be, and that should feel their *European* ground or groundlessness. Matthias's coda holds that awareness open to the potential of further grounding without defensively retrenching language and a feeling for institutions within the older code. Its crashing sound, an enigmatic *rappel à l'ordre,* and its quietly open stance, hopeful while blinking at nothing, are no one's thesis and anyone's, therefore exemplary.

About the tenet of untransferable linguistic meaning among poets of Bernstein's slant, I would align it, on nonlogical grounds, with the assumption that "out there" and "in here" convene in an omnipresent, neutrally colonized, wave-particle and scale-dissolving buzz, which lends to poetic agency a playground secure from "formally active" claims and hegemonies. It is slyly self-protective. Against this stand have mounted other pressures—global and corrosive to most category separations—which prompt a depth psychologist, Sherry Salman of New York, to write: "The prevalence of apocalyptic imagery that abounds in contemporary culture may be due in large part to the fact that there is simply no longer an out in which to banish or sequester what is unwanted" (166). That goes for more than poetics and language, to be sure. The inward or centripetal tendency as such is not in my sights, rather it is a covertly antinomian and nominalist turn.

My quarry in its narrowest sense is the poet's attitude when a *volte face* onto the zone of language's own life and functioning becomes necessary. Ever since the breakup of Aristotelian poetics, grounded in genres and affects, this turn has been a permanent tendency. The medical rethinking of topos and chora in Dr. Plotz can stimulate a poet's thinking in this wise, because it cannot abandon either the elusive phenomena nor those who variously suffer them, neither the sliding uncontainable facts nor the slippery pathos of experience. And that means holding in a single complex of oppositions both the detachment of the observer, or vocational observer, with the care of the bearer-and-feeler, a care that crosses those boundaries and distinctions which the observer must establish in order to function at all.

And here I turn again to my rough parallel from Late Antiquity, at the beginning of a recognizably modern consciousness about time, identity, and rhetoric. The Augustinian regrounding in a nonmaterial, nonspecific topos anticipates most subsequent reflective turns in that direction. First, a flip-flop occurs across categories, between place and nonplace, whose tension remains part of the revised experience. Also, in that tension, care is felt as the reply to anxiety and disorientation, although this care or love may be as paradoxical as the tension, just as Augustine's address to God goes unanswered. (Simone Weil sustained this paradox.) Finally, subjective experience and specific destiny (the sufferer's anamnesis being a special case of these) sustain the symbol of grounding in its unfolding, as distinct from a given place.

That unfolding takes time. In Matthias's work one can see the turn from eye to ear already in the double sonnet on Gruenewald and Hindemith's opera. There, however, the handmaiden of acoustics is a courage capable of free-fall. Matthias has come in the "Diptych" to a different pairing, of acoustics with illusionless love. That is one way of summarizing the thrust of his poem's long coda. And en route to that coda blows the dry but containing, paradoxically mothering wind of Rousillon. It removes inessentials, the moisture of passing thought and feeling, preserving only what abides. So, too, does the munitions blast remove any cobwebs in the ear for illusionless care.

Therewith a developing phenomenology for regrounding becomes legible in Matthias's poems: first comes ground as care in "A Wind in Rousillon," then an attempted regrounding in "Northern Summer," where chiastic flip-flops between eye-void and heraldic combinations-in-field move Matthias to separate reflective movement from rooted moves. Only in "A Compostela Diptych" does the movement toward regrounding reach full amplitude. The forays into crafty auditions of one's own poems and their poetics in *Revolutions* and its radical antecedent "An Automystifical Plaice," along with the subtly Mahlerian "Kedging in Time," almost as partners in divination, carry that movement into the workings of one's own language, in any final audition.

In closing, a differentiation. These reflections on the hyperspace that is home to a regrounding for poetic speech might be partly assimilated by students of Heidegger to his concept of the Earth, which antedates or outdistances being, opening a chasm in it, but is also the closure, hiddenness, or silence in anything that discloses itself. Nonhistorical, secretly consistent, nourishing but forgotten, the occulted basis of *dwelling*, it is also the secure enclosure of great art whose culture has passed away. To the extent that the inner ground of poetic speech stays silent about a cultural force or achievement while the poetry may be preoccupied with it, my notion parallels Heidegger's encompassing idea. But it goes no farther, which is quite enough. Poetic speech is mysterious, a radiant darkness whose ongoing power derives from the dead while facing into the future. Nostalgia and the higher museum instincts remain irrelevant. If writing stays awake, not dreaming some blackbird flight through language, it tends toward inner ground polarized by the dead and the unborn. That grounding looks ahead; Heidegger's Opening to Being and Derrida's termination of Western history and metaphysics ("We believe this literally") are radically prospective, but Carl Jung's long experiment in his notebooks, finally achieving full publication by 2020, demonstrate the interior foundations of such grounding. More than that I dare not report, being both ignorant and suspicious, an unwholesome combination.

Meanwhile, Matthias's parallel and repeated progressions make good sonar in that vasty cave where the poet actually conducts business. Oh blessèd nonplace of our meeting! No need to construct or deconstruct its foundations, for *there is no single place*. And memory is alive, not fixed—it persists yet self-distills, ongoing while remaining vulnerable. In these modes, memory is about as nostalgic as a trumpet voluntary or a munitions blast. Once we host memory in these ways, we will not suppose that it sits there like a bump on an analog. The end of given paradigms does not mean that paradigmatics has ended as a living form of thought. Supreme values have continued to go to hell in the same way, from Malraux's smashingly articulate youth to the present, in ways to which Derrida's announced literalism fails to do justice. Not that Matthias's poems populate their space and hyperspace with candidates for such supremacy. They cannot, for their ambition is to retain contact with what stays *in* the ground of the topos, not simply on the beloved and wind-torn ground underfoot, though beloved it surely is—an ambition that may seem modest until one places it in its time.

ABBREVIATIONS

BA Beltane at Aphelion
SM Swimming at Midnight

BIBLIOGRAPHY

Archambeau, Robert. *Revolutions. A Collaboration.* With John Matthias and Jean Dibble. Loveland, OH: Dos Madres, 2017.

Augustinus, Aurelius. *Confessions.* Translated by Henry Chadwick. New York: Oxford University Press, 1992.

Basso, Keith. *Wisdom Sits in Places: Landscape and Language among the Western Apache.* Albuquerque: University of New Mexico Press, 1996.

Bateson, Gregory, and Mary Catherine Bateson. *Angels Fear: An Investigation into the Nature and Meaning of the Sacred.* London: Rider, 1987.

Bernstein, Charles. *A Poetics.* Cambridge, MA: Harvard University Press, 1992.

Brown, Clarence. *Mandelstam.* Cambridge: Cambridge University Press, 1973. See esp. chapter 14, "Here Writes Terror: Poems, 1921–1925" and chapter 8, "1925–1938: Silence, Prose, Arrest, Exile, Sickness, Death."

Bruns, Gerald. *What Are Poets For? An Anthropology of Contemporary Poetry and Poetics.* Iowa City: University of Iowa Press, 2012.

Bunting, Basil. *Collected Poems.* London: Fulcrum Press, 1970.

Davenport, Guy. "Ernst Mach Max Ernst." In *The Geography of the Imagination: Forty Essays*, 373–384. San Francisco: North Point Press, 1981.

Davie, Donald. *Collected Poems*. Edited by Neil Powell. Manchester: Carcanet, 2002.

Hadot, Pierre. *The Veil of Isis: An Essay on the History of the Idea of Nature*. Translated by Michael Chase. Cambridge, MA: Belknap/Harvard University Press, 1976.

Harpham, Geoffrey. "Late Jameson." *Salmagundi* 111 (1996): 213–32.

Heidegger, Martin, "On the Essence of Ground" ("Der Satz vom Grund"), translated by William McNeill, 97–135. In *Pathmarks*, edited by William McNeill. Cambridge: Cambridge University Press, 1998.

Jones, David. *The Sleeping Lord and Other Fragments*. London: Faber & Faber, 1974.

Jung, C. G. "A Study in the Process of Individuation" [1939]. In *Collected Works*, v. 9.1. *The Archetypes and the Collective Unconscious*. 2nd ed. Translated by R. F. C. Hull. Princeton, NJ: Princeton University Press, 1969. πs 525ff.

——. "Concerning Mandala Symbolism." In *Collected Works*, v. 9.1. *The Archetypes and the Collective Unconscious*. 2nd ed. Translated by R. F. C. Hull. Princeton, NJ: Princeton University Press, 1969. πs 630ff.

Kandel, Eric. *In Search of Memory: The Emergence of a New Science of Mind*. New York: W. W. Norton, 2006.

Lesser, Wendy. *Music for Silenced Voices: Shostakovich and His Fifteen Quartets*. New Haven, CT: Yale University Press,.

Liscomb, Kathlyn. *Learning from Mount Hua: A Chinese Physician's Illustrated Travel Record and Painting*

Theory. Cambridge: Cambridge University Press, 1993.

Mandelstam, Osip. [See also Clarence Brown above.] *The Complete Critical Prose and Letters*. Edited by Jane Gary Harris. Translated by Jane Gary Harris and Constance Link. Ann Arbor, MI: Ardis, 1979. See esp. "Conversation about Dante" [complete; Clarence Brown's earlier translation in *Arion* is incomplete], 397–451.

———. "The Horseshoe Finder: A Pindaric Fragment." Translated by Steven Willett. *Arion* 9.2 (2001): 90–93.

———. "Whoever Finds a Horseshoe." [Poem 136, Moscow, 1923]. In *Complete Poetry of Osip Emilevich Mandelstam*, translated by Burton Raffel and Alla Burago. Albany: SUNY Press, 1973.

Matthias, John. *Beltane at Aphelion: Longer Poems*. Athens, OH: Swallow, 1995.

———. "After Five Words Englished from the Russian," *Revolutions: A Collaboration*. With Jean Dibble and Robert Archambeau. Loveland, OH: Dos Madres, 2017.

———. "Afterword" [with a selection of eighteen poems]. In *Five American Poets: An Anthology*, edited by Michael Schmidt and Clive Wilmer. Manchester: Carcanet, 2010.

———. *Kedging: New Poems*. Norfolk: Salt Publishing, 2007.

———. "The Poetry of Roy Fisher." In *Contemporary British Poetry: Essays in Theory and Criticism*, edited by James Acheson and Romana Huk, 35–62.

Albany, NY: State University of New York Press, 1996.

———. *Revolutions: A Collaboration*. With Robert Archambeau and Jean Dibble. Loveland OH: Dos Madres, 2017.

———. *Swimming at Midnight: Selected Shorter Poems*. Athens, OH: Swallow, 1995.

Munro, Eleanor. *On Glory Roads: A Pilgrim's Book about Pilgrimage*. New York: Thames and Hudson, 1987.

Nägele, Rainer. "The Poetic Ground Laid Bare (Benjamin Reading Baudelaire)." In *Walter Benjamin: Theoretical Questions*, edited by David Ferris, 118–38. Stanford, CA: Stanford University Press, 1996.

Partridge, Eric. *Origins: A Short Etymological Dictionary of Modern English*. London: Routledge and Kegan Paul, 1958.

Pindar. *Pindar's Victory Songs*. Translated by Frank J. Nisetch. Baltimore, MD: Johns Hopkins University Press, 1980.

Pinkney, Tony. "Modernism and Cultural Theory." In *The Politics of Modernism*. London: Verso, 1989.

Plotz, Paul, M.D. "Deconstructing Disease: An Anatomy of Illness in the Age of Molecular Biology." *Perspectives in Biology and Medicine* 40:20 (winter 1997): 160–64.

Pound, Ezra. *The Cantos*. London: Faber & Faber, 1975.

Redfield, James. "Herodotus the Tourist." *Classical Philology* 80 (April 1985): 97–118.

Ricoeur, Paul. *The Symbolism of Evil*. Translated by Emerson Buchanan. New York: Harper and Row, 1967.

Sallis, John. "The Policies of the Chora." In *The Ancients and the Moderns*, edited by Reginald Lilly. Bloomington, IN: Indiana University Press, 1996.

Salman, Sherry. *Dreams of Totality: Where We Are When There's Nothing at the Center*. New Orleans, LA: Spring Journal Books, 2013.

Tarn, Nathaniel. "The Heraldic Vision: A Cognitive Model for Comparative Aesthetics." *Alcheringa*, n.s., 2:2 (1976): 23–24. (special issue: Ethnopoetics: A First International Symposium, edited by Michel Benamou and Jerome Rothenberg).

———. *Views from the Weaving Mountain: Selected Essays in Poetics and Anthropology*. Albuquerque, NM: University of New Mexico Press, 1991.

Warminski, Andrzej. *Readings in Interpretation: Hegel, Hölderlin, Heidegger*. Minneapolis, MN: University of Minnesota Press, 1987.

ABOUT THE COLLABORATORS

JOHN MATTHIAS has published some thirty books of poetry, translation, criticism, and scholarship. For many years he taught at the University of Notre Dame, where he is still Editor at Large of *Notre Dame Review*. Shearsman Books publishes his three volumes of *Collected Poems*, as well as the uncollected long poem, *Trigons*, his most recent volume of poetry, *Complayntes for Doctor Neuro*, two books of memoirs and literary essays, and the novel *Different Kinds of Music*. Two of his long poems appeared in the last Dos Madres collaborative volume (with Archambeau and printmaker Jean Dibble), *Revolutions*.

JOHN PECK has published ten books of poetry, including *Contradance* (University of Chicago Press, 2011), *I Came, I Saw: Eight Poems* (Shearsman, 2012), and *Cantilena* (Shearsman, 2016). He taught English at Princeton, Mount Holyoke, the University of Zurich, and Skidmore, edits and translates for the Philemon Foundation (co-translator of Jung's *Red Book* and the forthcoming *Black Book*), and practices Jungian analysis in Maine.

ROBERT ARCHAMBEAU is a poet and literary critic whose books include *Home and Variations* and *The Kafka Sutra* and critical studies *Laureates and Heretics*, *The Poet Resigns: Poetry in a Difficult World* and *Inventions of a Barbarous Age: Poetry from Conceptualism to Rhyme*. He studied with John Matthias at the University of Notre Dame in the 1990s and has taught there and at Lund

University in Sweden. He now teaches at Lake Forest College. A new book, *The Valley of Saying: Poetry and Uselessness from Coleridge to Ashbery,* is due soon from Routledge.

KATIE LEHMAN is a freelance editor based in Bloomington, Indiana. While her focus is primarily on academic manuscripts, she has also worked with specialized and trade publications. She holds an MFA in poetry from the University of Notre Dame, and her poems have appeared in such publications as *Great River Review* and *CMW Journal.*

OTHER BOOKS BY JOHN MATTHIAS
PUBLISHED BY DOS MADRES PRESS

REVOLUTIONS (2017)

FOR THE FULL DOS MADRES PRESS CATALOG:
www.dosmadres.com